YOUTH AND CULTURE
for OCR

TRADE JUSTICE

John Richardson

Acknowledgements

Page design	Caroline Waring Collins (Waring Collins Ltd)
Cover design	Tim Button (Waring Collins Ltd)
Graphic origination	John A Collins (Waring Collins Ltd)
Graphics	Kevin O'Brien (Waring Collins Ltd)
Author index and typing	Ingrid Hamer
Reader	Mike Kidson

Picture credits

Photofusion 4 (ml, mr, bl), 6 (tl), 25 (b), 27 (tl, br), 32, 43; Rex cover, 4 (bl), 6 (tr, br), 8 (tl), 10 (bl), 12, 13, 14 (bl), 15 (ml, bl), 19, 20, 23, 24 (br), 25 (t), 26, 28 (bl, mr), 29, 35 (br); TopFoto 8 (br), 10 (br), 11, 14 (br), 22, 34, 35 (bm).

Cartoons

The cartoons in this book have been specially drawn by BRICK www.brickbats.co.uk

British Library Cataloguing in Publication Data
A catalogue record for this book is available from the British Library.

ISBN-10: 1-902796-71-3
ISBN-13: 978-1-902796-71-0

Pearson Education
Edinburgh Gate, Harlow, Essex CM20 2JE

First impression 2005
Printed and bound in Great Britain by Waring Collins Limited, Lancashire.

Contents

YOUTH AND CULTURE

Introduction

At one time or another you've probably heard someone say 'youth is wasted on the young'. It's usually spoken in jest but at the same time it reflects our mixed attitudes towards youth. On the one hand we see it as a time of thrills, excitement and fun. No wonder older people frequently envy the energy and vitality of the younger generation. However, there is also a 'troubled' side to youth. The enjoyment can be spoiled by worries about popularity, exams and jobs.

In this book we shall explore the highs and lows of being young. The highs of being a member of an exotic youth subculture. The lows of getting into trouble with the law. And not forgetting the everyday, humdrum routines that take up so much of young people's time – it's not all life on the edge!

One of the aims of this book is to show how the experience of youth varies across social groups. It makes a difference whether you are working class or middle class, male or female, Black or White. Also, youth culture takes on new forms with passing time. Growing up in the new millennium is so different in many ways from growing up in the 1960s. These variations show there is no simple answer to that perplexing question: what is it like to be young?

activity1 images of youth

questions

1 What images of youth are reflected in these photos?
2 Suggest three more images that would provide a fuller picture of young people in Britain today.

Unit 1 *Youth*

keyissues

1 Is youth biological or social?
2 What is the definition of 'youth'?

1.1 The social construction of youth

As we grow older, certain biological changes take place in our bodies. Babies develop the strength and coordination to walk. Somewhere around the early teens, children undergo the physiological transformations of puberty and enter adolescence. Youths mature into adulthood, ending in the slow physical decline of old age.

These biological changes are usually accompanied by changes in our attitudes and behaviour. Indeed, some scientists think that it is biology which largely accounts for these changes. For example, they claim that it is the hormonal changes of the teen years which make young people so restless, irritable and unsure of their identity.

But sociologists argue that these social changes are not just a result of our 'biological clock' ticking away. Rather, they are shaped to a large extent by the culture of the society we live in. In sociological jargon, youth is *socially constructed*.

When sociologists say that youth is socially constructed, they simply mean that it is affected by social and cultural factors. Youth does not mean the same thing in all places and at all times. For example, young people might act in a rebellious way in one society, yet act in a conformist way in another society. Different societies organise 'growing up' in different ways.

Anthropology and youth

Evidence for the social construction of youth can be found in anthropological studies of pre-industrial societies. These studies indicate that youth is partly a reflection of social values and customs.

Initiation rites Not every society has a 'youth' stage. In many cases there is a rather dramatic transition from childhood directly into adulthood. Usually this follows an initiation ceremony which marks the change in status. These ceremonies are *rites de passage* (rituals that mark a passage from one status to another). In these initiation ceremonies the young people are usually separated from the rest of their tribe for a short period in order to undergo training and prepare them for their adult roles and responsibilities. The training may include tests of courage and endurance, or physical operations such as circumcision or scarring. After successfully completing this ritual they are welcomed into adult society. In Western societies, by contrast, there are few clear lines or ceremonies to mark the passage to adulthood.

Storm and stress? Adolescence in Western societies is often regarded as a time of 'storm and stress' – teenage mood swings, emotional turmoil and a restless search for identity. But Margaret Mead's study (1928) of growing up in Samoa suggests this is not inevitable. She argued that the simplicity of Samoan society provides a peaceful transition to adulthood, unlike Western societies where young people are faced with agonising choices between conflicting sets of values and standards. She claimed Samoa is a remarkably relaxed society, and children make the transition to adulthood with a minimum of fuss. Mead concluded that the differences between Western and Samoan youth show the importance of culture rather than biology. (However, it should be pointed out that her description of Samoan society has been challenged, and she may have overstated her case).

Table 1 *Perspectives on youth*

Biological approach to youth	Social construction of youth
Youth is a result of biological growth.	Youth is a result of social and economic changes.
Youth is much the same everywhere in the world.	Youth varies between different cultures and societies.
Youth is a time of turmoil and problems, caused by biological changes.	Youth simply reflects social and cultural conditions.

Adapted from Muncie, 1999

activity2 initiation

Item A Chisunga

The Chisunga ceremony among the Bemba people of Zambia marks a girl's passage to womanhood. It takes place soon after her first period and involves a number of rituals, including physical ordeal, social isolation and ceremonial singing. The ceremony lasts for about a month, after which she is taken out of isolation, bathed and dressed in new clothes. The Chisunga prepares girls for marriage, teaches them the secrets of Bemba women, and is designed to make them 'grow' and become 'women'. At the end of the ceremony, girls are considered ready for marriage and a marriage ceremony often follows immediately.

Adapted from A.Richards, 1982; quoted in Pilcher, 1995

Item B Changing status

Students graduating, Manchester University

Passing her driving test

questions

1 In what way is the Chisunga ceremony an initiation ritual?

2 Can the activities shown in Item B be regarded as initiation rituals?

activity3 the difficult years?

Item A Happy teenagers

A British survey has found that most young people aged 13-18 get on with their parents. This challenges the popular image of sullen teenagers locked in their room after endless family rows. The idea of teenagers rebelling was probably more true of the 1960s.

85% of the sample agreed with the statement 'I'm happy with my family life'.

A majority said their lives were 'happy', 'fun' and 'carefree'.

Only 1 in 10 said they did not get on with their parents. The most common family flashpoints were 'tidying up' and 'household chores'.

Adapted from *The Observer*, 6.10.2002

Item B Kevin and Perry

Kevin and Perry (Harry Enfield and Kathy Burke)

questions

1 In what ways does Item A challenge Mead's distinction between Samoan and Western youth?

2 What image of youth is suggested by Kevin and Perry?

History and youth

Further evidence for the social construction of youth is found in history. Some historians claim that childhood and youth are relatively recent 'inventions' of the past few centuries.

The invention of childhood The French historian Phillipe Aries (1962) argued that childhood as we know it never really existed in the Middle Ages. After the age of about 6 or 7, infants were treated as miniature adults, without any intervening stage of childhood or youth. It was only around the 15th century that the more modern view of childhood as a period of 'innocence' and 'dependence' slowly began to appear. Over the following centuries children were gradually withdrawn from the labour market and enrolled in formal education. Childhood became a more extended period of life and it became more sharply separated from adulthood.

The emergence of youth According to some historians, youth began to be recognised as a separate life stage in the late 18th century, after the 'discovery' of childhood. The distinction between childhood and youth remained quite blurred for a long time. But gradually youth became recognised as a stage somewhere between childhood and adulthood. However, Roberts (1997) states that, even as late as the early 20th century, there was no over-arching youth culture in Britain. Even between the two World Wars the dance halls, cinemas, sports venues and pubs were aimed mainly at adult customers. It was only in the 1950s and 1960s that a confident youth culture emerged.

The social construction of youth – conclusion

It would be foolish to deny that biology plays some part in 'making' young people. For example, puberty is a major landmark in a person's sexual development. But even so, society channels young people's sexuality in various ways. For example, in Britain young people are physically capable of having sex a few years before society considers that behaviour legally and morally acceptable.

Further evidence that youth is socially constructed comes from anthropological and historical evidence. This evidence indicates that youth is not ruled solely by the 'biological clock'. Our journey through life is a social and cultural journey just as much as a biological one.

1.2 Defining youth

It is not easy to say what we mean by the term youth nowadays. Some people see it as the teenage years. Others link it to adolescence (a term coined in the early 20th century to refer to the emotional troubles that accompany puberty). Probably the simplest solution is to see it as the stage between childhood and adulthood. But where exactly does childhood end and adulthood begin?

Childhood

Some say childhood ends with the arrival of puberty. But the age of puberty varies for different people, it is usually earlier for girls than boys, and it seems to be occurring earlier for everyone. Another solution is to say childhood ends with the arrival of 'adult' rights. The United Nations Convention on the Rights of the Child defines a child as any person below 18 years old. But legal rights are given at all sorts of different ages (see Table 2).

Table 2 Legal rights

Age	Legal right
10	Age of criminal responsibility
13	Take part-time employment
16	Leave full-time education
16	Buy cigarettes
16	Legally engage in consensual sex
17	Drive a car on public roads
18	Vote
18	Marry without parental consent
18	Get tattooed
18	Buy alcohol in a pub
21	Adopt a child

*activity*4 *loss of innocence?*

Item A *Mad about boys*

A new magazine, *Mad About Boys*, aimed at girls aged 9 to 12, has been criticised for encouraging young girls to dress sexily.

The magazine is advertised as being 'full of real-life hunks – a dozen dream dates for you', and implores readers: 'Be gorgeous. Make sure you'll be looking your dazzling best when you meet that perfect boy'.

Michelle Elliot, the director of the charity Kidscape says: 'The magazine features a sweet little girl who looks great until they make her up to look like a French tart. We are pushing young girls into being sexual, putting them in tight skirts and make-up, making them aware of their bodies in a way which is unhealthy'.

Adapted from the *Independent*, 7.2.2001

Item B Growing up fast

question

In what ways do these items confirm Postman's views? (See below.)

Item C Acting older

Disappearance of childhood? Some experts fear that childhood itself is disappearing in the modern age as children are prematurely pitched into the adult world. Neil Postman (1983) complains that the mass media expose children to uncensored adult messages from a very early age and so they rapidly become confused little adults. These 'tweenagers' abandon children's games in favour of pop culture, they imitate sexy adult dress styles, and they start drinking and smoking at an early age. Postman believes these trends are responsible for the rise in the numbers of children committing crimes.

Adulthood

If it is difficult to judge where childhood ends. It is equally hard to identify the beginning of adulthood. At one time, it might have been dated from getting your first full-time job or settling down into marriage. But nowadays, youth is being 'stretched' – young people are studying for more prolonged periods and marrying later in life. As a result, full adulthood is being delayed.

Youthfulness Perhaps it is the 'youthful', carefree attitude of youth that makes them different from adults? But evidence

activity5 youthfulness

Item A Forever young!

Patsy and Eddy

Item B Softball

Over 60s softball match

Item C *Staying young!*

Helen Murray, 35, businesswoman 'Although I've got a child and a high-powered job, I don't feel grown-up or in control of my life. Being grown-up is not necessarily a positive thing anyway because when you stop growing maybe you begin to stagnate.'

Phil Armfield, 40, inventory analyst 'At work I act like a grown-up because I'm trying to project a sensible and mature image, but once I'm out of the building, I can be myself again and say: "Bugger it, I'm going to enjoy myself and worry about it later".'

David Sumpter, 32, software engineer. 'I don't feel any need to "grow up" and settle down and have kids – I can do all that when I'm 45.'

Interviews by Michael Cooke, quoted in Beaumont, 1996

question

What do these items suggest about youthfulness?

doesn't always bear this out. Many adults retain their 'youthfulness' well into middle age and even longer. Indeed, Berger (1971) argues that youthfulness is a personal quality, an attitude to life rather than a matter of age. Not all young people are 'youthful', and many 'youthful' people are not young. Regardless of their biological age, youthful persons tend to be impulsive, spontaneous, energetic, playful, and thrill-seeking.

Defining youth - conclusion

The boundaries of youth seem to be shifting. Youth appears to be arriving earlier (with the 'disappearance' of childhood) and lasting longer (with the postponement of jobs and marriage).

key terms

Social construction of youth The social and cultural shaping of youth attitudes and behaviour.
Adolescence Teenagers in the post-puberty phase, a period thought to be associated with emotional problems.
Puberty The stage at which people acquire certain sexual characteristics (hormonal changes etc).

So nowadays, it is quite common to use the term to apply to a wide age range – usually the 16-24 year-olds. Some researchers even use the 13-24 age band. Obviously this is a highly diverse group – the lives and interests of 13 year-olds are hardly the same as those of people in their early twenties.

summary

1. Biological explanations assume that biological and physical characteristics are major factors in shaping the behaviour of youth.

2. Social constructionists argue that youth is largely shaped by social and cultural factors. This accounts for the wide variations in their roles over time and across societies. Indeed, youth – and youth culture – seem to have emerged relatively recently in Western society.

3. There are no clear initiation rites for youth in countries like Britain. Moreover, the boundaries of youth have been moving in recent years. The trend is for youth to become 'stretched' – to begin earlier and last longer.

Unit 2 *Youth culture and subcultures*

keyissues

1 What is youth culture?

2 What are the main kinds of subcultures?

3 How do young people use drugs?

Youth culture

It was only in the 1950s and 1960s that a recognisable *youth culture* appeared in Britain. Its appearance had a lot to do with the social circumstances at that time:

- Young people were spending longer periods in education and this gave them greater opportunities to develop a culture of their own.

- Young people were able to find jobs relatively easily and this boosted their spending power. They spent their money on new clothes, hair styling, make-up and transport (motor bikes, scooters).

- The expanding leisure and entertainment industries started to cater for young people's tastes. They provided meeting places (eg, coffee bars, clubs) for youngsters and they produced the music young people wanted to hear.

- In the 1960s, society seemed to be changing at a rapid pace. Young people were seen as playing a key role in the dynamic new society.
- The 1960s were a time of sharp social conflicts (eg, the Vietnam War, anti-racism struggles). Many young people flocked to the *counter-culture movements* that emerged around those conflicts.

Youthquake As young people became more affluent, they started to cultivate their own styles of dress, music and behaviour. Groups such as the Teddy Boys and Mods seemed to have values and lifestyles that diverged sharply from the rest of society. Leech (1976) warned of a 'youthquake' which was opening a huge culture gap between young people and their elders. This gap was probably exaggerated because of the excessive publicity given to unruly and rebellious youth. Nevertheless, the rise of youth culture marked an important social trend. Young people seemed to be developing a special 'world' of their own, one in which they carved out their own values and lifestyles. The values they celebrated were mainly those of leisure, fun, excitement and rebellion.

Youth subcultures

The term youth culture implies that every young person follows the same lifestyle and subscribes to the same set of values. But youth culture is actually composed of a number of different *subcultures*. A subculture can be defined as a culture within a culture. The members of a subculture participate in the common culture of the society but they also possess some distinctive cultural features.

Table 3 *Youth subcultures*

Subculture	Dominant drug/music/style
(1950s-1970s)	
Teddy Boys	Alcohol; rock 'n' roll; Edwardian dress
Mods	Amphetamines; soul; Italian style, scooters
Rockers	Alcohol; rock 'n' roll; leathers; motor bikes
Skinheads	Alcohol/amphetamines; ska; boots 'n' braces
Hippies	LSD/cannabis; progressive rock; Eastern styles
Rastas	Cannabis; reggae; dreadlocks
(1970s-1980s)	
Punk	Amphetamines; punk; DIY mixtures
Metal Heads	Alcohol; heavy metal; denim
New Romantics	Amphetamines; glam rock; sexual blurring
(1980s-1990s)	
Acid House	Ecstasy; poly-drug use; garage/techno/ trance/ambience
Rave	Gangsta rap/jungle/drum 'n' bass/garage/ bhangra

Adapted from Muncie, 1999

activity6 conforming and non-conforming

Item A *Conforming*

A Barnardo's survey of young people aged 13-19 has found that they are highly conformist and conventional in their attitudes. They feel drug use at school should be punished, they don't believe people should get married while very young, or leave school too early or have sex below the age of consent, and almost a third support film censorship laws.

Adapted from Roberts & Sachdev, 1996

Item B *Non-conforming*

Skinheads

Punks

question

What would the people in Item B be likely to think about the views expressed in Item A?

Drugs, sex and rock 'n' roll A number of subcultures have burst onto the scene over the last 50 or so years (see Table 3). It is not always the case that one subculture replaces another – they may co-exist and overlap. Some fade away while others enjoy revivals. Sometimes they enjoy a harmonious relationship, sometimes they are locked in conflict. The 'flower power' philosophy of hippies may have disposed them to love others but skinheads did not always return the affection!

Mapping subcultures

Sociologists and journalists have described the changing styles and values of youth subcultures over the years. But more attention has been paid to 'exotic' subcultures than to 'ordinary' youth.

Conventional youth At any given time, the majority of young people are probably 'conventional' in the sense that they enjoy many of the pursuits of youth culture but do not fit in to any particular group. For these 'respectable' youngsters, school and work may be just as important as subcultural style and attitude. Yet this group has been neglected by researchers. Sara Delamont (2000) notes that there are few studies of 'ordinary' young people who go to evening classes or run Brownie packs. She also accuses sociologists of an anti-intellectual bias – they study low-brow popular culture (eg, *Top of the Pops*) and ignore young people who like classical music or archaeology.

Exotic subcultures The attention of sociologists has focused mainly on the more spectacular and exotic youth subcultures. These groups seem to be more successful in commanding the wider loyalties of their followers. Each participant seems to be a dedicated member of a single, distinct subculture with its own values, style and 'uniform' (eg, hippie beads, the biker's leather gear). Members of these expressive subcultures seem to be making a cultural statement about themselves. They express their identities through their dress, music, appearance and behaviour.

Goths

Paul Hodkinson's study (2002) of Goths helps us to understand a lot about youth subcultures. According to Hodkinson, Goths fulfil the four main requirements to be considered a subculture.

- They have a firm sense of their own identity (they see themselves as insiders and look down on outsiders).
- They have a commitment to the group (it influences their everyday lives).
- Their style is consistent enough to somehow 'hang together' (it is easy to recognise Goth style, even if there is some internal diversity).
- They have a relatively high degree of independence (to a large extent they produce their own books, fashion and music).

Goth style Subcultures are usually associated with a particular style and appearance. The Goth style emerged in the early 1980s from its origins in punk and glam rock. Goths are one of the most immediately recognisable subcultural groups. The characteristic look is 'black' and 'feminine' for both sexes. They wear black clothes, black hair (usually back-combed), and vivid facial make-up, often set against a whitened face. Also popular are ripped fishnets, crucifixes and body piercings (earrings, nose rings), and fetish gear (rubber, PVC, dog collars) worn for artistic rather than sexual purposes. Females often wear velvet tops, corsets and frilly tops. Goths use a lot of horror imagery, and their musical taste tends to be melancholic and macabre.

activity7 being a Goth

Item A Goth scene

In your own words, please explain what the Goth scene is all about.

'Being different to all the mindless, brain-dead clones that walk around small-town England.'

'The clothes, the style – the general interest in things that are dark and macabre.'

'It's about dressing up in your best stuff and listening to great music.'

'We enjoy the books, films, music and clubs.'

Adapted from Hodkinson, 2002

Item B Goths

Dressed up to see Marilyn Manson

questions

1 What does Item A tell us about the attractions of Goth subculture?
2 What sort of 'statement' do you think the photo makes?

Goth subculture Hodkinson, himself a Goth, has made a detailed study of this subculture. He says it is mainly about style rather than any sort of rebellion. People participate because they enjoy the music, the fashions, and companionship with others who share their tastes. Hodkinson says there is much to appreciate about Goth culture. For example, there is very little violence or sexism, and both male and female followers kiss and touch each other freely and without embarrassment. Even though it waned a bit in the mid-1990s, there is still an active cult following. They maintain their own networks by running conventions, producing fanzines and flyposters, keeping in touch through the Internet, and seeking out Goth-type clubs wherever they can find them.

Rave culture

Rave culture is only part of what is more generally called dance culture or club culture. Bennett (2001) explains that the roots of contemporary dance music lie in two musical innovations: house (where 'mixing' produces new sounds and tones) and techno (computerised and electronic technology). It was these innovations that led to the popularity of dance cultures in the late 1980s and 1990s.

The scene According to Muncie (1999), rave is essentially a combination of dancing at mass all-night events, synthesised techno music with a heavy repetitive beat, and the use of Ecstasy pills. The stars are the DJs who sample tracks to play for the dancers. Fans of the scene claim that the atmosphere is typically friendly, non-sexual and non-threatening. However, rave culture attracted some notoriety after the tragic death of Leah Betts who had a fatal reaction to Ecstasy. Also, in the late 1980s the police clamped down on ravers who met in unlicensed venues and warehouses,

and so the scene shifted to more regular commercial clubs.

Subcultural capital Sarah Thornton (1995) describes how insiders try to show how 'cool' they are by dressing, dancing and talking in the right way, and by showing their superior taste in music. This *subcultural capital* (being 'in the know') is destroyed if dancers are seen to be trying too hard! The coolest ravers place heavy stress on being 'authentic' (recorded music is seen as better than 'phoney' live music), 'hip' (preferring the cool rave scene to superficial mainstream music) and 'underground' (an alternative to the commercial scene dominated by mass media).

Drugs cultures

Youth culture is often linked with the excessive consumption of drugs. This reputation is probably deserved as far as tobacco and alcohol are concerned. Although tobacco consumption has declined among the general population over the past twenty or so years, it has dropped less sharply among young people. During the same time, teenage drinking has increased. Drinks manufacturers have been criticised for exploiting the teen market by marketing alco-pops drinks (sweet-tasting but powerful drinks, usually vodka-based). These are seen as one of the reasons for the upsurge in 'binge' drinking where large amounts of alcohol are drunk in a short time.

'Normal' drug use Howard Parker et al. (2002) have run several surveys among young people in the North of England. The conclusion they draw is that drug use has become a normal part of youth lifestyles. Youngsters often begin binge drinking in their teens and continue this pattern into their early 20s. Also, soft drugs such as

activity8 raves

Item A *Glazey*

Glazey: For me, part of going out to raves is to do the drugs and smoke a bit of pot. The music and the drugs definitely go hand in hand. The people at all-nighters all want to have a good time and dance and meet people. It's not like getting pissed and coming on to some woman. There's a real group feeling there. There's no bad vibes, it's all good vibes, and that's probably to do with Es and the feelings they generate. Y'know, you feel totally safe at these events.

But the worst thing about it is going to work at 7.30 on a Monday morning. Especially if I've been smoking all day Sunday and not managed to get any sleep. That's a killer!

Adapted from Garratt et al., 1997

question

What do these items tell us about the attractions and pitfalls of raves?

Item B *Fatboy Slim*

200,000 people at a free concert given by Fatboy Slim on Brighton beach

cannabis have become an everyday regular feature of their social scene. Although these drugs are illegal they have become 'normalised' within youth culture. Drug use is common among males and females and across all social classes. Drugs are readily available, young people 'know' about them and have usually tried a number of them. However, Parker et al. found that recreational drug use is generally handled in a sensible fashion. Although most young people know of others who use cocaine and harder drugs, only a minority use them.

Table 4 *Drug use and young people*

Use of drugs in last year by 16-24 year-olds, 1998, England and Wales
(percentages)

	Males	Females
Cannabis	32	22
Amphetamines	12	8
Ecstasy	6	4
Magic mushrooms	5	2
LSD	5	2
Cocaine	4	3

Adapted from *Social Focus on Young People*, 2000

Youth culture and subcultures – conclusion

The term youth culture was coined to capture the new spirit among young people in the second half of the 20th century. This culture has many admirable features. Indeed, Osgerby (1998) says modern youth can be congratulated for turning Britain into a more moral and tolerant society, with less sexism and racism than in the past.

It soon became clear, however, that youth culture consisted of a number of different subcultures. Researchers have given most attention to the more exotic subcultures. These subcultures have special attractions for their members. This was illustrated in the case of Goths and ravers.

As society changes, so new subcultures arrive on the scene and old ones fade away. But subcultures have maintained a problem reputation, especially for things like risky drugs behaviour.

key terms

Youth culture A term used to describe the distinctive cultural values and lifestyles of youth in the post-war period.
Counter-culture movements Movements which are actively opposed to some of the aspects of the mainstream culture.
Subcultures Sub-groups within cultures. They share in the wider culture but also have some distinctive cultural features.
Subcultural capital The 'inside' knowledge of a subcultural scene that establishes the credibility of 'cool' members.

activity9 drug abuse?

Item A *Prince Harry*

Item B *Drinking*

question

Do these items suggest that drug use has become 'normal' among young people?

summary

1. Youth culture emerged in the later decades of the twentieth century. Youth were becoming more independent and were beginning to forge their own values, lifestyles, tastes and fashions.

2. Within youth culture there are a number of subcultures, each with its own particular characteristics. Subcultures are expressive – they express different sets of tastes and values. Some subcultures have a distinctive dress code and set of rituals. More conventional youth are less committed to any one subcultural style, but they sometimes borrow ideas and fashions from the more exotic groups.

3. Subcultures change over time, reflecting the changes in society. Some flamboyant subcultures (eg, Goths) still exist, but the dance scene has been more prominent in recent years.

4. Youth have a bad reputation for binge drinking. Howard Parker's research suggests that youth have a wide knowledge of illegal drugs but mostly avoid the harder drugs. Soft drugs have become a normal feature of the youth scene, and they are usually handled in a sensible fashion.

Unit 3 Youth divisions

keyissues

1. Are youth subcultures divided along class lines?

2. Do young men and women have different subcultural styles?

3. What is different about ethnic subcultures?

Early commentators on youth culture frequently made two mistakes. The first mistake was to exaggerate the gulf between youth culture and adult culture. Youth culture was never a totally self-contained little world on its own. The second mistake was to assume that youth culture was much the same for all youth, regardless of their social backgrounds. Gradually, it became clearer that the social origins of young people – their class, ethnicity and gender – had a strong influence on their subcultural activities and experiences.

Class subcultures

Myth of classlessness In both Britain and the United States some sociologists speculated that youth culture was 'classless', with young people from all classes mixing freely in the same clubs and listening to the same music. But Murdock and McCrone (1975) showed that 'pop culture' in the 1970s was divided into sub-styles that ran along class lines. Working-class youngsters were attracted to reggae, soul and mainstream pop, while middle-class youth preferred 'alternative' and 'progressive' sounds. Also, middle-class youth were more likely to join counter-culture movements such as peace groups. They were also more likely to belong to 'bohemian' groups centred around alternative and artistic lifestyles.

Class protest Many of the early youth subcultures saw themselves protesting against the injustices of society. But this protest took different forms according to the social class of the members..The middle-class hippie solution, for

activity10 spot the class

Item A Live 8

Item B Football fans

question

Can you guess the social class of these people?

example, was to drop out of the ruthless capitalist system and follow a lifestyle based on 'flower power' (peace, love, sex, drugs and rock 'n' roll).

This solution contrasts sharply with the response of working-class skinheads to their subordinate role in society. Phil Cohen (1972) interpreted skinhead culture as a rather desperate attempt to defend working-class values in a society which held them in low esteem. Skinheads showed their defiance through an exaggerated celebration of traditional working-class styles (eg, overalls, braces, boots,

short hair) and values (eg, manliness, toughness, physical strength).

Class convergence? Many of the early youth subcultures had class links. The Teddy Boys and skinheads were mostly from working-class backgrounds. Many Mods were working class youths heading in an upwardly mobile direction towards routine white collar jobs. But the connection between class and subculture is not always tight. For example, punk music attracted working-class youth but it was also inspired by middle-class youths in art schools.

activity 11 hip-hop style

Item A Endorsements

G Unit trainers worn and endorsed by the rapper 50 Cent and marketed by Reebok are named after 50's rap collective, G Unit. S. Carter trainers, also marketed by Reebok, are named after Shawn Carter, better known as Jay-Z. Sales of these trainers have rocketed, according to Reebok, because of their association with rap stars. Other companies have followed suit. Missy Elliott has been featured in Gap commercials and Adidas ads, and Virgin Mobile has used Busta Rhymes in its ads.

Adapted from *The Observer*, 30.11.2003

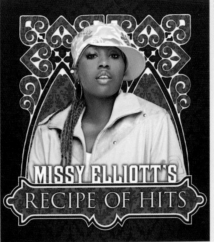

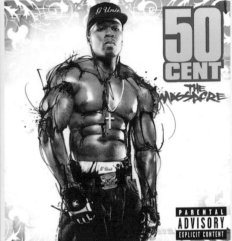

Item B Eminem

Item C Ali G

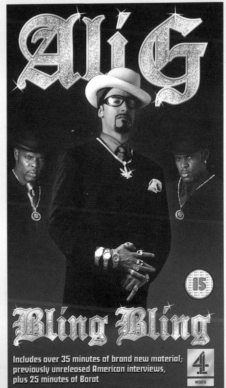

Item D A global style

Chinese hip-hop fans in Beijing

question

What do these items suggest about the popularity of Black style?

Roberts (1997) believes that the class boundaries between subcultures have blurred over the years. Nowadays there is less class segregation. Different social classes often attend the same sorts of clubs, engage in similar leisure activities and display the same tastes and styles. But Roberts believes most young people still carve out their leisure lifestyles within the boundaries of their class. Also, he points out that class still has a strong effect on the educational and employment prospects of young people. There are signs of some convergence in leisure tastes and styles, but middle-class youths enjoy many advantages in other aspects of life.

Ethnic subcultures

Minority traditions Young people from ethnic minorities participate in and enjoy many of the mainstream youth pursuits in Britain. But they also have their own cultural traditions of music, dress and dance. In some cases, they may feel their ethnic subcultures are more relevant, attractive and satisfying. Or they may have little choice (eg, young Asian females can move more freely within Asian peer groups). Another factor is the constant threat of racist abuse or violence. In response to this, young people from ethnic minorities sometimes prefer to develop their own youth styles. Expressing their own identities and lifestyles is a way of defying racism and asserting their independence.

Black youth subcultures The Rasta culture of the 1970s is a good example of a distinctive Black style that evolved in part as a response to racism. The Rasta style revolved around dreadlocks, Ethiopian colours (red, green and gold),

and reggae music. Ganja (cannabis) was regarded as a sacred weed, but Rastas disapproved of alcohol and gambling. Rasta style had some influence on skinhead and punk musical tastes but its appeal to Whites was limited by its association with a Black identity and religious creed.

This stands in sharp contrast to the huge popularity of hip-hop culture, with its mixture of rap, hip-hop and R&B music. Rap with its 'gangsta' lyrics based on street life in the 'hood' and its aggressive macho sentiments has now been incorporated into mainstream pop culture.

Asian youth subcultures Until quite recently few White people in Britain were aware of a youth culture among Asians. But that is changing. Bennett (2001) describes the rising popularity of bhangra (a blend of Indian folk music with Western pop) among Asians in Britain. A few years back the bhangra musicians had a bit of an image problem – they were too old, over-weight and all-male. So young people have taken bhangra and developed it further, fusing it with other musical traditions (eg, ragga is a blend of bhangra with rap and reggae). According to Bennett, these 'cross-over' developments have played a major part in the formation of new Asian youth identities.

Gender subcultures

Osgerby (1998) argues that postwar social change probably transformed the lives of girls more deeply than those of boys. Admittedly they were still more likely than boys to be closely supervised by parents and to do housework chores. But they had greater freedom than before and they set out to have fun with great spirit and energy. Girls were as

*activity*12 *feelings*

Item A Bottling it up

(young woman) 'I can talk to my close friends about anything. We're always having deep and meaningful conversations.'

(young man) 'I don't find it easy to talk about my feelings with my friends. They could take the mick and go telling everyone what you've been saying.'

(young woman) 'Women find it a lot easier to talk to other women, are a lot more open about their feelings – men try and bottle it up, try to be hard. Boys have to look macho and can't show their true feelings – that's easier for girls.'

(young man) 'Women show their feelings more, they can talk to someone close but men keep it all inside.'

Adapted from Bradford & Urquhart, 1998

Item B Taking the mick

questions

1 What does Item A reveal about gender differences among youth?

2 Suggest reasons for the reaction of Gary's friend in Item B.

prominent in Mod culture as they were in the later Goth and rave scenes. Yet, curiously, early studies of British youth subcultures focused mainly on males, and girls were either ignored or described as mere hangers-on at the fringes of boys' groups. Slowly, however, feminist researchers started to pay more attention to girls.

Bedroom culture Feminist researchers showed that gender makes a difference. For example, McRobbie and Garber (1975) suggested that girls have best friends, whereas boys socialise in larger groups. And girls typically met and chatted about personal matters in the bedroom rather than on the male-dominated street. In the feminine bedroom culture of the 1960s and 1970s, girls played records, practised dance steps, experimented with clothes and make-up, and talked about romance, boyfriends and marriage.

Girl power Later research indicates important changes since the 1960s and 1970s. There are some signs of gender convergence (eg, nowadays young people often have friends of both sexes). Also, McRobbie (1991) reports that teenage magazines for girls (eg, *Just Seventeen*) no longer restrict themselves to romance and boyfriends. They seem to accept that their readers are also interested in fashion, pop music, personal problems and future careers. Girls are now portrayed as strong-minded, independent and assertive. Some researchers even talk about 'girl power'. One example of this is the rise of the so-called ladette, the female counterpart of the lad. The ladette seems equally willing to booze, swear and indulge her sexual appetites.

Boys Some commentators argue that boys are becoming a 'lost generation' unsure of their masculine roles in a fast-changing society. Some evidence for this *crisis of*

activity 13 *teen mags*

Today's magazines for teenage girls are obsessed with sex: confessional ('I fell in love with a nun'); boasting ('Sex in the bath: a deliciously dirty experience') and cautionary ('I was filmed having sex'). There are also features on how exactly to do it, including 'Position of the fortnight' in *More* and tips on oral sex in *TV Hits* magazine. This has so alarmed Parliament that it has passed a law to set up a Teenage Magazine Arbitration Panel. In 1998, this panel ruled that a feature in *Sugar* ('I slept with 40 boys in three months') breached this code, as did an article in *Bliss* ('My teacher is my lover').

Adapted from Tucker, 1998

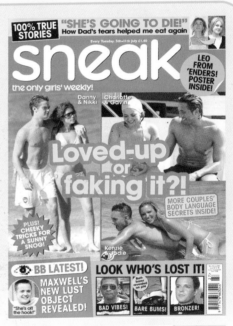

question

In what ways can these magazines be seen as an example of ladette culture?

masculinity is provided by Adrienne Katz (1997) who has conducted surveys of large samples of 13-19 year olds in Britain. She identifies a high number of 'can-do' girls bursting with self-confidence and optimism and ready to compete on equal terms with males. But the rise of girl power seems to have sapped the confidence of some boys. They often feel confused (eg, told to 'act like a man' but also expected to have tender feelings).

On the other hand, some researchers claim that young men welcome the new freedoms offered in a less sex-stereotyped society. They get pleasure from what was previously seen as a feminine interest in clothes, hair and personal appearance. Also, they can relax the macho image and express their feelings with less fear of ridicule.

Youth divisions – conclusion

A great deal of youth culture is shared by people from all walks of life. In the 1960s and 1970s most people enjoyed the Beatles and the Rolling Stones. But your social origins and background do make a difference to what you select from youth culture and what themes you find most relevant.

Admittedly, many of these differences have diminished over the years. Furlong and Cartmel (1997) conclude that the relationship between class and youth cultures has all but vanished, and gender differences have been weakened.

The trends are less clear-cut as far as ethnicity is concerned. Asian bhangra music has not really achieved mainstream popularity. Black hip-hop culture, on the other hand, has had a big impact on mainstream youth style.

key terms

Bedroom culture The feminine youth style centred around meeting in one another's homes rather than on the street
Hip-hop A 'Black' style which combines rap, hip-hop and R&B.
Crisis of masculinity An insecurity and uncertainty about masculine identity and roles.

summary

1. Young people share the most popular parts of youth culture but they also develop particular subcultural styles in order to suit their class, gender or ethnic tastes and interests.

2. Some youth subcultures in the past were dominated by a particular social class. Nowadays youth subcultures are less firmly identified with social classes.

3. Gender differences in youth subcultures were most visible in the bedroom culture of girls. Gender differences still exist (eg, boys are less likely to discuss intimate matters with friends). But contemporary subcultures (eg, club cultures) are far less gender divided than in the past.

4. Ethnic subcultures are formed for a number of reasons. Sometimes the ethnic subculture is a defiant response to racism. In the case of hip-hop culture, however, the ethnic style has proved immensely popular with White youth.

Unit 4 Theories of youth subcultures

key issues

1 What functions do youth cultures perform for young people?
2 How do radicals and feminists explain youth subcultures?
3 How are subcultures changing in the postmodern age?
4 What risks do youth face?

Why do youth subcultures emerge? What problems do they solve or create? What makes them change? In this unit we shall examine some leading explanations for these sorts of questions. For a long time functionalist theories dominated the field until they were challenged by radical and feminist theories. These rival explanations take up the first section of this unit. The second section deals with the newer postmodern and risk theories.

4.1 Order and conflict

Functionalist theories

Functionalists see society as a giant system that works because its various parts support one another (just in the same way as the organs and limbs of a body pull together). Each part of the system has a function – it makes a contribution to other parts. This can be applied to youth and youth cultures. Functionalists seek to identify the functions that youth culture performs not just for its members but for the wider society.

Socialisation In modern industrialised societies there is a wide gulf between childhood and adulthood. So functionalists such as Talcott Parsons (1954) argued that these societies need to create a special stage of 'youth'. Young people are segregated in specialised institutions of education and training so they can undergo a prolonged period of socialisation. In this way, they slowly learn the complex and sophisticated skills and values that prepare them for adult jobs and responsibilities. The segregation of youth is functional for society as a whole because it allows the cultural heritage and shared values to pass smoothly from one generation to the next.

Identity Youth in modern society occupy a sort of limbo land, neither fully children nor fully adults. As a result, they are often confused about their identities. Functionalists argue that youth culture has important

activity14 sexual recklessness

The sexual behaviour of our teenagers has now reached such levels of recklessness and damage that it is becoming a horror story running out of control.

There has been a huge increase in promiscuity and consequently in sexually transmitted diseases (chlamydia, gonorrhoea, syphillis) which can permanently impair fertility or trigger other health problems.

What is lacking is not advice about sex or contraception but a moral context. Teenagers are immature and need adult guidance.

Adapted from Melanie Phillips, *Daily Mail*, 28.6.2002

question

How does this article cast doubt on functionalist views of youth culture?

Members of True Love Waits, a pressure group for sexual abstinence among young people before marriage

functions here. It provides young people with the support of a peer group while they try to 'find themselves'. Youth culture is a collective solution to their problems. It helps them to feel understood (they share common lifestyles) and it gives them a sense of power and control. In the course of experimenting with different styles and new identities, they gradually mature and 'grow up'. So youth culture helps them to develop stable personalities and this prepares them for the responsibilities of adulthood.

Criticisms The functionalist argument seems to make a lot of sense but it is weak at certain points. It is pitched at too general a level – the experience of growing up varies according to the class, ethnicity and gender locations of young people. Functionalists also exaggerate the separateness of youth culture – young people are not cut off from the rest of society to the extent that functionalists imply. Finally, functionalists seem to assume that everything works out for the best. Radicals take a different view, seeing youth cultures as a form of protest against exploitation and injustice.

Radical theories

In the 1970s and 1980s the Centre for Contemporary Cultural Studies (CCCS) developed radical theories of youth subcultures. They were radical in the sense that they were highly critical of the class inequalities found in capitalist societies. But the novelty of the CCCS approach was the way it allied this interest in class with a detailed study of the styles and symbols of youth culture.

Resistance The CCCS writers (eg, Jefferson, 1975) saw working-class youth subcultures as a form of resistance against a class-divided society. One of the unusual things about this resistance was that it was largely *symbolic*. It

was mainly through their subcultural styles that these youths expressed their protest – *resistance through rituals*. So the CCCS researchers set out to interpret the underlying meanings of the symbols and rituals employed by the new youth subcultures. For example, the bizarre gear of punks (eg, swastikas, safety pins) seemed designed to challenge and undermine 'respectable' values. The aggressively masculine behaviour of skinheads was interpreted as an exaggerated defence of traditional working-class male lifestyles.

Space A common CCCS argument was that working-class youth were trying to win some *cultural space* for themselves, a space where they could defend and assert themselves. By creating new subcultures with their own meanings, rituals and identities, working-class youth refused to accept other people's low opinion of them. But Phil Cohen (1972) pointed out that this symbolic resistance was a 'magical' solution (ie, it only gave the appearance of being an effective solution). It did not succeed in abolishing class inequalities in wealth or power. Also, when the new styles of music, dress and dance were copied by lots of other people in society, the rebellious subcultures began to appear a bit tame rather than subversive.

Criticisms Perhaps too much was read into these subcultural styles. How many of the participants would have recognised the rebellious motives attributed to them? Dick Hobbs (1988) found that skinheads were more interested in fashion than in solving some class struggle! So a more obvious explanation for the attractions of these subcultures is that they were *fun*. Also, the CCCS researchers tended to focus on the more dramatic and colourful youth subcultures. Class divisions may not be so visible among the mass of 'ordinary' youth.

activity15 carnival against capitalism

A long day of carnival and peaceful protest against capitalism turned into a riot yesterday as demonstrators wrecked parts of the City of London and fought with police. The Carnival was organised on the Internet and it attracted jugglers, clowns, anarchists, musicians and all sorts of activists. The participants included the Biotic Baking Brigade (famous for throwing custard pies at celebrities). Revellers danced, sang and partied as they staged their demonstration.

Adapted from *Daily Telegraph*, 19.6.1999

Anti-capitalist protestors

question

In what ways does the Carnival resemble 'resistance through rituals'?

Feminist theories

One of the criticisms levelled at the CCCS studies was that they neglected young women. But feminist researchers have since tried to fill in the gaps. The discovery of the bedroom culture is one example. Early feminist research made two main points. First of all, gender makes a difference – males and females have different subcultural styles. And secondly, girls tend to be disadvantaged, at every class level, compared with boys.

It's different for girls Sue Lees (1993) interviewed pupils aged 15-17 in some London inner-city schools. She was particularly interested in the way they developed gendered identities. The boys in her study were scared to appear soft and feminine and so they quickly learned that they had to resort to hard language and avoid the sort of intimate talk which they associated with girls. Girls, on the other hand, feared being identified as slags and so they cultivated softer ways of talking. They also took a great deal of care over the way they dressed (stylish enough to be sexually attractive but not so extreme as to be thought loose or easy). Lees argues that this detailed attention to physical appearance is not so much a 'natural' feminine thing but rather something that girls are taught.

Patriarchy Feminists argue that male and female are not just 'different' – they are also unequal in the sense that males have greater power. This male power is called *patriarchy*. For example, in the schools studied by Sue Lees there was a sexual 'double standard'. If a girl went around with different boyfriends or engaged in intimate sexual behaviour, then her reputation was damaged. But if a boy behaved the same way with girls his reputation was enhanced!

Criticisms If the CCCS researchers can be criticised for focusing on males, then feminist researchers have sometimes been guilty of the opposite bias. This may have been justified when there were few studies of female youth subcultures. But nowadays it is important to get a balanced picture in order to see whether gender differences have declined. It may no longer be the case that boys are more privileged. Indeed, some feminists have moved away from highlighting female subordination towards a celebration of female achievements over the last decade or so.

Order and conflict – conclusion

Functionalists celebrate the 'good' side of youth subcultures. But radicals stress the underlying injustices that drive working-class youth to stylish protest. They say these subcultures are telling us that something is wrong with society. Feminists add something else to the picture. The struggle is not just about class – it is also about gender.

Obviously, it is important to be aware of the weaknesses of each of these theories. But they all add to our understanding in some way, even if they occasionally overstate their case.

key terms

Functionalism The view that the social and cultural parts of a society contribute towards its overall stability and survival.
Function The contribution that the part makes to the whole of society.
Resistance through rituals A protest against social injustice, in the form of styles that are different from, and opposed to, those of the majority.
Cultural space A 'space' in which people are able to express, assert and defend themselves.
Patriarchy The power of men over women.

activity16 boys as victims

Item A A cry for help?

There is a strong resistance to viewing boys as unhappy victims. Yet the anxiety felt by teenage boys is genuine. One minute he hears scorn being poured on 'new men' for being insufficiently sexy. The next he hears contempt for displays of laddishness. He doesn't know what is wanted of him.

Even when boys engage in acts of masculine bravado, it is as much about desperation as power. Often it is a cry for help.

As a society, we have been too willing to swallow feminism's insistence that all males are powerful rather than vulnerable.

Adapted from Ros Coward, *The Guardian*, 16.3.1999

Item B Who am I?

questions

1 Why is Item A sceptical about the notion of patriarchy?

2 How does the cartoon illustrate Item A?

4.2 New theories

Postmodern theories

Postmodern theories highlight the diversity and fragmentation of youth culture in the postmodern age. The boundaries between subcultures have become very blurred. Indeed, the old 'solid' subcultures are no longer possible, since young people now follow lifestyles based on their individual tastes.

Supermarket of style Youth subcultures in the past seemed to be stable and distinct. People from the same neighbourhood, school or social class usually adopted the same subcultural style and followed it for a number of years. The old subcultures were 'authentic' in the sense that they were based on consistent meanings and values (eg, 'rebellion'). But that is changing. Nowadays we are faced with a 'supermarket of style' (Polhemus, 1997). The golden age of subcultures has passed because nowadays there are simply too many choices and options. Admittedly there are certain 'styletribes' with distinctive fashions (eg, ravers, cyberpunks, New Age travellers). But Polhemus insists that young people are less committed to one particular style and they are reluctant to give themselves subcultural labels.

Pick 'n' mix Young people nowadays are more likely to adopt a casual pick 'n' mix approach to style. They play with different looks and styles, sampling and mixing them in all sorts of unexpected and imaginative ways (eg, Gay Skinheads, Bikers for Jesus). Sometimes they revive old styles (eg, Mod, punk) and blend them with contemporary styles. The point is, they make their choices on an individual basis, purely on the grounds of whether it suits their current lifestyle and cultural tastes and preferences.

For example, Sarah Thornton (1995) argues that club cultures are 'taste cultures' – the only thing that brings ravers together is their shared taste in music.

activity17 style supermarkets

We now inhabit a Supermarket of Style where, like tins of soup lined up on endless shelves, we can choose between more than fifty different styletribes...You name it, we've got it. You too can be an anarchic Punk, a bohemian Beatnik or a bad ass Raggamuffin. If only for a day.

Adapted from Polhemus, 1997

question

What is 'postmodernist' about this supermarket of style?

Criticisms Sometimes postmodernists exaggerate the differences between the past and the present. Perhaps the old subcultures were not quite as fixed and stable as they imagine. Also, distinct youth subcultures have not entirely disappeared in the present day – Goths are one example.

Risk theory

Risk theory claims that risk is a central concern in contemporary society. In previous societies risks were largely 'natural' (eg, bad harvests, earthquakes) but nowadays they are often the result of social complexity and technological development. Cieslik and Pollock (2002) believe risk theory helps us to understand many of the problems of youth today. The number of risks has multiplied in contemporary society. There are so many choices to make. These choices are difficult because the outcomes are unpredictable. Moreover, youth culture does not always help young people to handle these risks – they are often left to make their own individual choices.

Youth transitions Risky choices have to be made if youth are to make a successful transition to adulthood. A *transition* is the process of moving from one stage of life to another. The transition from youth to adulthood involves a number of changes (see Figure 1). In modern society this transition stage has been extended (eg, people are studying longer and marrying later). It also throws up more choices (eg, the choice between cohabitation and marriage). And for some young people it is becoming more difficult. They may become 'trapped as teenagers' because they cannot find work or cannot afford to leave the family home and set up their own household.

Figure 1 Youth transitions

	Youth		Adult
Economic	school	→	work
Domestic	family of origin	→	marriage/cohabitation
Housing	parental home	→	own home

Getting a job

In the 1960s most young people landed a job on leaving education. But the youth labour market collapsed in the 1980s and 1990s (partly because the introduction of new technology lowered the demand for unskilled labour). Educational and labour markets were restructured and youth increasingly found themselves faced with a bewildering maze of routes and pathways from which they had to choose. These included youth training schemes (eg, the New Deal), modern apprenticeships, and a variety of educational courses (eg, A levels, NVQ, access courses). Nowadays the path to work is longer, more complex and fragmented. The jobs themselves are often temporary, insecure and precarious. So young people have to be prepared to re-train and move around the job market. They keep having to make choices, and the risks are high.

activity 18 Status Zer0 youth

There are surprisingly high numbers of young people aged 16 and 17 who have no visible means of support. They are not in education, training or employment. They arrive at Status Zer0 in a host of different ways (broken homes, unexpected homelessness etc). They live from day to day, with money a constant worry. Many slip into benefit fraud, casual 'illegal' work or petty crime. Their daily round is lying in bed until late, wandering around shops (and possibly shoplifting), hanging around in the evenings (and possibly using drugs and drinking) and staying up until the early hours.

Adapted from Williamson, 1997a

Homeless and hungry

question

What 'transitions' have these young people failed to make?

Eating disorders

Making a transition can be stressful. Sometimes this expresses itself in eating disorders such as anorexia (starving yourself) and bulimia (bingeing on food then making yourself sick). Today there are lots of cultural pressures to be slim (eg, waif-like models in glossy magazines parade the 'glamour' of being thin). Many young people are obsessed with their body weight and shape. But only a minority develop eating disorders. However, these disorders appear to be on the rise. They are most common among females (about ninety per cent of sufferers). The risk is greater at points of transition (the sexual transition of puberty, and the transition from education to work). One popular explanation is that sufferers attempt to exert control over their bodies when they feel they cannot control other aspects of their lives.

Criticisms Risk theory perhaps overstates its case. Were previous societies really any less risky than present-day

activity 19 feeling the stress

Item A Food abuse

Ellen has well-off parents, attends a public school and has won sporting honours at hockey and rowing. But none of this has protected her from food abuse. 'Looking back I think my problems started when my mum and dad were having lots of arguments. Also, a gang of girls at school were picking on me. It all became too much for me.'

In many respects girls' problems are the same as always: self-esteem, independence, money, good looks and coolness. But the pressures are even worse nowadays. They have to be seen to be doing the right thing, wearing the right clothes, hanging out with the right friends. They are victims of the 'Perfect Girl Syndrome'.

Adapted from *Independent on Sunday*, 6.10.2002

Item B Jodie Kidd

Item C Getting lighter

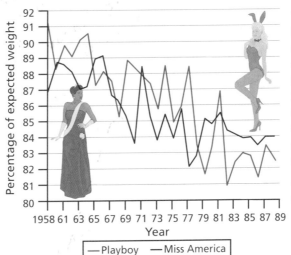

This graph shows the average body weight of Miss America contestants and *Playboy* centrefold models from 1959 to 1989 as a percentage of their expected weight in terms of age and height. Over 60% weighed 15% or more below expected weight which is one of the criteria for anorexia.

Adapted from Wiseman et al., 1992

questions

1 What 'risks' does Item A reveal?
2 How do Items B and C illustrate cultural pressures to be slim?

---

societies? Also, how much choice do young people really have? Furlong and Cartmel (1997) say young people today may have the *impression* of greater freedom but in fact their lives are still restricted by their social class position. Finally, risk theory portrays a world full of threat and hazard – but many young people may not see it that way. Youth can be a time of adventure, optimism and excitement.

New theories – conclusion

Postmodern theories draw attention to some key trends. Bennett (1999) even claims that subculture is a term that no longer applies to modern youth. He suggests it should be replaced by the term *neo-tribe* – a loosely organised grouping with no fixed membership and no deep commitment. Nowadays, he says, lifestyles are increasingly individual and based on fleeting tastes.

Risk theory also touches on key developments in modern life. As Kenneth Roberts (1997) says, it is now more difficult for young people to know the kinds of adults they will become. They cannot avoid taking risks, and they often have to make their own individual decisions rather than following in the footsteps of their friends or parents. However, Roberts notes that uncertainty is not always experienced as a threat. Some people enjoy the freedom to choose.

key terms

Transition The process of moving from one stage of life to the next.
Neo-tribe or styletribe A loose grouping around shared style or tastes, with fleeting and flexible membership.

summary

1. Functionalists see youth culture as having positive benefits for young people at a difficult and uncertain time of their lives. They also see the prolonged period of youth as contributing to the overall stability and efficiency of society. It gives young people time to build the confidence and skills necessary for performing adult tasks.

2. Radicals see working-class youth subcultures as a form of protest against the injustices and inequalities of capitalist society. This protest takes the form of style rather than politics. By reading what young people are trying to say through their styles, we begin to understand that youth subcultures are really forms of resistance.

3. Feminists introduce the idea that youth subcultures are gendered – boys and girls adopt different styles and roles within youth groups. Moreover, they argue that girls are often forced to take subordinate roles to boys.

4. Postmodernists argue that the 'old' subcultures have splintered and frayed. Rather than belonging to a single subculture, young people move freely between different style groups, mixing them with little difficulty. Lifestyle choices are made on an individual, rather than group, basis.

5. Youth can be seen as a process in which young people are constantly moving closer to adulthood. The idea of transitions helps us understand many of the difficulties faced by youth.

6. Risk theories argue that youth transitions are increasingly complex and risky. Some young people enjoy the uncertainty but for others it can bring problems.

Unit 5 *Youth and delinquency*

keyissues

1 Is the 'deviant' reputation of youth exaggerated?

2 What are the main patterns of delinquency?

3 How does delinquency vary by class, gender and ethnicity?

Trouble

There is a long history of seeing young people as a highly 'deviant' group. Geoff Pearson (1983) describes waves of public outrage against rowdy and unruly youth ever since the 19th century. In the 1890s there were fears about 'hooligans'. In the 20th century attention switched to the razor gangs of the 1930s, the Teddy Boys of the 1950s and the Mods and Rockers of the 1960s. Pearson notes that every generation has voiced identical fears about youthful troublemakers, seeing them as a symbol of social breakdown and moral decline.

Moral panics

Many young people get into a spot of bother with the law, and some cause severe harm. But often the extent and seriousness of youthful misbehaviour is exaggerated. Stan Cohen (1987) calls this a *moral panic* – an excessive reaction to some perceived trouble.

activity20 *pictures of youth*

Item A *The hooligan*

At twelve—his literary education

At seventeen—a full-fledged Hooligan

From the *Daily Graphic*, 5.12.1900

Item B *Football fans, Euro 2000*

Item C   Teenagers

question

What image of youth is reflected in these pictures?

Mods and Rockers Cohen's study of Mods and Rockers in the 1960s shows how these youths were portrayed in sensationalist terms. The media circulated misleading and alarming stereotypes about them (eg, that they were habitually violent). This stoked public fears and led to an escalation of social control measures. Police restricted their movements and dance halls refused them entrance simply because of their bad reputation. Cohen says this over-reaction led to *deviance amplification* – it actually made things worse and created more deviant acts. For example, Mods and Rockers sometimes fought with the police when they felt they had been treated unfairly.

Later panics Cohen believes that moral panics keep being created because societies need to make sense of social change, especially if it is seen as a threat. This helps to explain why there have been so many moral panics since the 1960s. Muncie (1999) describes how moral panics have been launched over a wide range of 'threats', including football hooligans, illegal rave parties, lager louts, New Age travellers, Asian gangs, and the crack and ecstasy drugs cultures.

Delinquency

Juvenile delinquency is a term that refers to criminal activity (eg, theft, vandalism, assault) by young people. But it is sometimes stretched to cover a range of anti-social misconduct as well (eg, youngsters 'making a nuisance' of themselves). Delinquency can be 'expressive' (done for excitement and thrills) or 'instrumental' (done for financial gain), or a combination of both. It is difficult to get accurate figures on crimes by young people, since not all offences are reported to the police or recorded by them. So some researchers use *self-report surveys* which ask people to declare if they have committed an offence, or been the victim of one, in the recent past.

Patterns of delinquency Newburn (2002) describes the broad pattern of crimes committed by young people:

activity21 bullying

Letter to Childline from a bullied young person.

'There is this girl who always teases me and provokes me and I hate it. When she does this my other friends just laugh and I pretend to laugh but I feel like crying. She has never hurt me physically but I think mentally is worse. Sometimes when I go home I cry. I really don't want to be friends with any of them any more but I don't think any one else would want to be my friend. Please could you write back and tell me what to do but disguise the letter so my mum does not find out.'

Adapted from Garratt et al., 1997

question

Can this sort of bullying be regarded as 'delinquency'?

- At least a quarter of all recorded crime is committed by 10-17 year olds, and over two-fifths is committed by those under 21. Moreover, self-report studies confirm that it is common for people to commit an offence in their teens.

- The peak age for offending seems to have risen in recent years, and it is currently around 18 for males and 15 for females. But it varies according to the particular offence (eg, for males it is 16 for violent offences but 20 for drugs offences).

- Property offences are still the most common type of offence but there has been a significant rise in drugs and violent offences since 1987.

- For girls under 15, the most common offences are criminal damage, shoplifting, buying stolen goods, and fighting. Over the age of 16, fraud and buying stolen goods are more common.

Victims Young people are themselves often the victims of crime. Boys aged 10 to 17 are at high risk of becoming victims of street crime, especially in London, and most of those who prey on them are around the same age. Today's schoolchildren have more valuable possessions, such as mobile phones, which make them an attractive target for muggers.

activity 22 taxed

A *Mirror* poll reveals a nation of youngsters who have been mugged for cash, mobile phones and clothes, slashed with knives and shot by airgun thugs. Under-16s are 50% more likely to become victims than the rest of the population. 1 in 5 has suffered a crime in the past 18 months. More than 2 in 5 are very worried or fairly worried about being a victim. Teenagers are so used to being robbed that they have their own slang term – being 'taxed' – for street robbery. Fewer than half the offences are reported to the police.

Adapted from *Daily Mirror*, 16.9.2002

question

Are young people justified in being worried about crime?

Class and delinquency

Official crime statistics indicate that most young offenders come from working-class backgrounds. This might be partly due to biases in the ways crimes are recorded (perhaps middle-class offenders are treated more leniently). But it would hardly be surprising if poorer groups are more involved in delinquency. Property crime offers a way of getting your hands on goods you could not otherwise afford. Violence or anti-social behaviour may be a way of striking back at a society that frustrates you. Power and Tunstall (1997) studied 28 violent disturbances ('riots') by White youths between 1991 and 1995 in 13 areas of Britain. Most of the rioters were young, male and unemployed. The riots occurred in low-income areas with long-standing social and economic problems.

The yob In recent years there has been a severe backlash against young men behaving like 'yobs'. Ros Coward (1999) describes some of the assumptions behind this backlash. The yob is usually stereotyped as a young, White, working-class male. He could be a lager lout, a football hooligan, or a joyrider. He is seen as foul-mouthed, irresponsible, unemployed and violent. Accompanied by his pit-bull terrier, he terrorises the locals in his council estate. He is often drunk, uses drugs and is heavily involved in crime. Coward admits that these young men do pose a problem but she feels they are being made scapegoats for social injustices. Seen from a distance the yob is a menace. Closer up, a more complex picture emerges of powerless young men struggling with difficult circumstances. Joyriding, fighting and vandalism may be ways of expressing 'manhood' when more respectable avenues (eg, decent jobs and income) are denied.

Gender and delinquency

Something like three-quarters of all young offenders are male. Indeed, Ros Coward and many other writers tend to view youth crime as a misguided attempt to express 'masculine' values. But perhaps this underestimates the numbers of female delinquents.

Female delinquents Some researchers suggest that a lot of female delinquents go unnoticed and there are far more of them than we realise. However, Maguire (2002) dismisses this argument. He says self-report surveys show that males are much more likely than females to admit to having committed offences such as burglary, car theft, and theft from vehicles. In addition, Heidensohn (2002) says that women commit a small share of all crimes, and, compared with males, these crimes are less serious and less likely to be repeated.

Nevertheless, female criminality is slowly on the increase and the gender gap has narrowed over the last thirty or so years. In 2001, for instance, girls overtook boys in shoplifting offences.

Ethnicity and delinquency

Juvenile delinquency is found among all ethnic groups. The *Youth Lifestyles Survey* (Graham & Bowling, 1995)

activity23 yobs

Item A Escape

Torched by joyriders

Joyriders and car thieves are hardly lovable people. But car theft and joyriding offer a temporary escape for young men who suffer poverty and unemployment. It is not only the speed which is a thrill, but the momentary sense of rising above the everyday hopelessness and meanness of inner-city life. The excitement helps them 'get away from it all'. It is a form of protest.

Adapted from Taylor, 1997

Item B Headlines

ONE MORE VICTIM OF OUR YOB CULTURE
A father of four was kicked to death by yobs after being asked for a light.

LOUTS DESTROY ANOTHER FAMILY
Britain's yob culture has claimed the life of yet another family man.

ATTACKED BY A TEEN GANG
A barrister was in a coma last night after becoming the latest victim of a teenage street gang. Yobs are intimidating entire neighbour-hoods.

Headlines from the *Daily Mail*, June and July 2005

questions

1 Compare Item A with Ros Coward's views.
2 What impression is being given by the headlines in Item B?

---

took a sample of over 800 young people and asked them about their offending. These self-report findings suggested that White and African-Caribbean youth had similar offending rates, and these were higher than those of South Asian youth. But the pattern of offences varied, with Whites more prominent in fraud, African-Caribbean and Indian youths more likely to steal from schools, and White and Pakistani males more heavily involved in vandalism.

Ethnic stereotypes Stuart Hall et al. (1978) describe how young Blacks were linked with 'mugging' offences in the 1970s. The mass media created a series of moral panics about mugging – a crude category that covers various 'street crimes' involving theft or robbery. They stereotyped Black youth as the main offenders, in spite of all the difficulties in deciding 'real' crime rates. These moral panics overlook the possibility that official statistics may be distorted by racial discrimination in the criminal justice system (eg, police may be more likely to 'look out' for Black offenders, and more likely to press charges).

Asian youth have been pictured as law-abiding and conformist, tightly controlled by the elders in their ethnic communities. For example, Ali Wardak (2000) found little

activity24 girl violence

A survey of 800 13-16 year olds in Scotland has found that teenage girls inhabit a violent world – 4 out of 10 have been beaten up by another young person, and 3 out of 4 say they 'frequently' witness violent incidents.

Louise, a 16 year old from Glasgow, said: 'There are a lot of girls who hang about the streets looking for trouble. It's frightening walking past them on your own because they shout abuse and call you names, trying to wind you up. If you shout back at them it's likely they will hit you.'

Her friend Claire, 15, said: 'We had to stop hanging around outside at nights because we were always getting chased by the girls. Often they would have metal poles or bottles. Once one of my friends was even threatened with a knife held up to her throat.'

Adapted from *The Independent*, 2.10.2000

question

In what ways does this challenge the view that delinquency is largely a male problem?

criminal activity among young Pakistanis in Edinburgh. But in recent years Asian youth have gained a more 'criminal' image. Back and Keith (1999) say young Bangladeshis in the Isle of Dogs have become the new *folk devils* in the eyes of the local population. They are seen to use weapons, fight unfairly and act 'flash'. Moreover, Asian youth have won a new 'violent' image after their participation in the riots that broke out in towns in northern England in the late 1990s and into the new millennium.

Victims Ethnic minorities run a greater risk than Whites of being victims of street crime and racial attacks. The most notorious case is that of Stephen Lawrence, an 18 year-old who was brutally murdered at a bus stop in Eltham, London in 1993. Subsequently the *Daily Mail* named five White youths as his killers but no successful prosecution has been secured in spite of trials, inquiries and an inquest. The Macpherson Report (1999) on the murder concluded that the investigation had been marred by a combination of police incompetence and institutional racism.

Youth and delinquency – conclusion

The first question is whether young people deserve their 'deviant' reputation. The answer to this is a qualified yes or no. Youths do account for a high proportion of all recorded crime. However, it is also true that most young people are largely conformist, and many youth offences are relatively trivial.

The second question is whether social concern about juvenile delinquency is out of all proportion to the actual problem. Stan Cohen's concept of moral panics alerts us to the possibility that this is often the case. But this does not deny the harm caused by crime.

Lastly, the official statistics (for all their flaws) do suggest there are class and gender patterns to delinquency. It is more difficult to draw conclusions about ethnic minority groups because of the possibility of racial biases and the operation of racial stereotypes.

key terms

Delinquency The criminal acts of young people.
Moral panic An exaggerated and often hysterical reaction to some wrongdoing.
Deviance amplification A process in which a misjudged over-reaction to deviance results in even more deviant acts.
Folk devils Groups who are (unfairly) seen as a threat to the rest of society.
Institutional racism The collective failure of an organisation to provide an appropriate professional service to people because of their colour, culture or ethnic origin.

activity25 villains and victims

Item A Black 'muggers'

BLACK CRIME: THE ALARMING FIGURES (*Daily Mail*)

THE YARD BLAMES BLACK MUGGERS (*Sun*)

YARD REVEALS RACE LINK IN STREET CRIME EXPLOSION (*Daily Express*)

LONDON'S STREETS OF FEAR (*Daily Mirror*)

Adapted from Gordon & Rosenberg, 1989

Item C Murder

Parents of Stephen Lawrence who was the victim of a racist murder in 1993.

Item B Riots

Bradford, 2001. One of the riots, mainly involving Asian youths, which broke out in Northern towns in 2001.

questions

1 Suggest how the headlines in Item A could be seen as part of a moral panic.

2 Suggest various ways of interpreting the picture in Item B.

3 There is a tendency to see Blacks as the perpetrators rather than the victims of crime. Discuss with reference to Items A and C.

summary

1. Concerns about juvenile delinquency are not new. It is difficult to say whether it is a bigger problem now than in the past. However, the official statistics do suggest that youths account for a high proportion of all crime. Much of this is relatively petty and trivial.

2. Juvenile delinquency does leave victims and so it should not be treated lightly. But societies sometimes over-react. These moral panics can sometimes lead to deviance amplification.

3. Official statistics must be treated with caution because of the biases involved in reporting and recording crime. But the statistics suggest that delinquency is more common among male working-class youths. However, female delinquency appears to be on the rise.

4. Different stereotypes attach to young people as far as delinquency is concerned. The 'yob' is seen as a menace to society, while girls are treated as 'naturally' law-abiding. Black youths have been labelled as 'muggers', while Asian youths have (until recently) been regarded as peaceful and conformist.

Unit 6 Youth gangs

keyissues

1 What is a gang?

2 What are youth gangs really like?

The idea of gangs has a firm grip on the public imagination. Films like *The Godfather* glamourise the Mafia, with its fixed membership, its strict hierarchy and its own code of values and behaviour. Delinquent gangs are sometimes thought to run along similar lines, even if their crimes are minor in comparison. We imagine they are well-organised groups with leaders, oaths of loyalty and a membership that is committed both to the gang itself and to its delinquent activities. But the truth is a bit more complicated, as we shall see.

activity 26 having fun

When they have been asked, delinquents put the pursuit of fun high on their list of reasons for misbehaving. Far from being miserable, they are enjoying themselves.

Adapted from Morgan, 1978

Joyriders

question

How does this fit in with Thrasher's view of the gang?

Youth gangs in the USA

The idea of youth gangs was popularised by Frederick Thrasher (1927), who studied a massive 1,313 gangs in Chicago. According to Thrasher, the gang emerges more or less spontaneously as young people compete for territory and resources. The gang members hang around together and plan their actions as a group. Out of this face-to-face interaction they gradually build a group tradition, a spirit of solidarity, an awareness of their group identity, and attachment to a local territory. Thrasher recognised that these gangs sometimes behaved in a reckless and unlawful manner but he regarded their activities as rather innocent. He thought they were based on a search for adventure and excitement, a result of the teeming energy of young males.

Delinquent subcultures Later researchers added further details on the youth gang. Albert Cohen (1955) developed the idea of a *delinquent subculture*, a way of life that has become traditional among boys' gangs. Some of these delinquent subcultures are 'versatile', engaging in a wide range of activities. But others specialise in particular activities such as fighting, drug-taking or theft.

The Latino groups that emerged in Los Angeles in the 1980s and 1990s do appear to have a tight gang structure, with clearly defined membership, their own 'colours', hand signals and rituals. But in many so-called gangs there is no fixed membership, and only limited agreement on roles and expectations. Most of the time their behaviour is law-abiding, and few seem totally committed to delinquency.

Youth gangs in Britain

Reports about youth gangs have a long history in Britain. Roberts (1971) describes the moral panic in the late 19th century over the notorious Northern 'scuttlers' who fought vicious pitched battles with rival gangs. Also, Geoff Pearson (1983) describes how, in the 1950s, Teddy Boys swiftly gained a bad reputation for gang fights, vandalism and riots in cinemas. In the 1970s and 1980s the media frequently reported gangs of football hooligans on the rampage. Patrick (1973) has identified organised fighting gangs in Glasgow, and Daniel and McGuire (1972) have described a skinhead gang (or 'mob') in the East End of London.

Territory One of the features that lends credibility to the idea of a gang is a sense of territory. Researchers have noticed how common it is for working-class youths to jealously guard 'their' territory against outsiders. Phil Cohen (1997) suggests that *territoriality* is a way for powerless and deprived groups of youth to create a sense of their own self-importance. They may have little control over things like jobs and money but at least they can physically defend 'their' patch.

Do gangs exist?

In spite of the popularity of the word, most British researchers believe 'gang' is a misleading term. Most so-called gangs are little more than loose and shifting *social networks* where lots of people come into contact with one another, but there are no clear members, no recognised leaders, and little consensus on values and behaviour. So the dominant view is that tightly-knit delinquent gangs are rare in Britain. Even in the case of Daniel and McGuire's skinhead 'gang', the group had no system of ranks or leaders. Everyone in the gang shared a similar lifestyle, but there were no rules as such.

Girls' gangs Researchers are particularly sceptical about sensationalist claims that girls' gangs are a rising threat. In recent years various commentators have claimed that organised girls' gangs are springing up all over Britain. It appears that the crime rates of young women are rising, but this hardly justifies the moral panic which has been whipped up by the media. The violent girl gang is largely a myth, according to a Department of Health Report,

Antisocial Behaviour by Young People. This report says that the reason for the growing involvement of girls in youth crime is partly because they are spending less time at home with parents and more time on the street. The 'bedroom culture' of young women is increasingly being replaced by a street corner lifestyle, and this is creating more opportunities for getting into 'trouble'.

The Milltown Boys

Howard Williamson's study (1997b) of the Milltown Boys has the great advantage of tracking a delinquent group over a long period of time. Williamson first studied the Milltown Boys in their deprived Cardiff housing estate in the late 1970s. He describes them as a social network rather than a structured gang, but he admits they had some gang-like features (eg, preoccupation with territory and rank). When they were in their mid-teens their behaviour was mostly law-abiding, if a bit wild and boisterous. They enjoyed 'aggro' (at football matches), daubing graffiti and just 'messing about'. Crime (theft) was largely casual and simply a way of getting some spending money. But gradually they got into stealing cars, working fiddles and committing burglaries. By the age of 18 they were frequently drunk, constantly picking fights, and regularly involved in criminal activity. Even in their early twenties, many were still 'trapped as teenagers'. Far from growing out of offending, their teenage delinquent lifestyle persisted.

Growing up After a gap of twenty years Williamson (2001) re-visited the Milltown Boys (now in their early 40s). By this time the original group of about sixty people had divided into three groups. The more fortunate ones had regular work and stable personal relationships and had become home-owners. Another group had frequent spells of unemployment and mixed fortunes in their personal lives. The remaining third had a 'duck and dive' lifestyle where they survived by drug-dealing, crime and signing on

activity27 Bitches with Attitude

Item A Girl gangs

Roweena is seventeen and heads an all-girl gang, Bitches with Attitude. She attended a private school until she was expelled for maiming another pupil she believed to be prettier. She rubbed lighted cigarettes into her rival's face, gave her a black eye and left her scarred after kicking her with a stiletto heel.

Playground bullying is now as likely to be carried out by girls as by boys, and the number of expulsions among girl pupils has increased dramatically. Girls have seen how an aggressive approach commands respect, and they imitate it. On the street, girls have become actively involved in robberies and the drug trade. Their street violence is often targeted on vulnerable women.

But although it is a growing problem, it must be remembered that women still account for only a minority of violent crimes.

Adapted from Brinkworth, 1997

Item B Crime, age and gender

Crime rates per 10,000 population, 2003

England and Wales	Age	
	10-15	16-24
Males	193	577
Females	78	116

Adapted from *Social Trends*, 2005

questions

1 What light does Item A shed on girl gangs?

2 Female crime should not be exaggerated. Discuss with reference to Items A and B.

for welfare benefits. Surprisingly, most of the Milltown Boys continued to live in the area and they still had fierce local loyalties. Although some of them were no longer active in crime, they had no qualms about buying stolen goods. Ironically, in light of their own backgrounds, many of them despaired about the 'little bastards' (young delinquents) in the area. They were also deeply concerned about the corrosive impact of the drugs culture on the community.

Ethnic minority gangs

Black youth in Britain have had a 'criminal' reputation ever since the moral panic over mugging in the 1970s. More recently, the rise of gangsta rap has made the public even more likely to associate Black youth with organised crime. Newspapers have printed alarming stories about the exploits of armed Yardie gangs in places like London and Manchester. In Birmingham in 2003, two young Black women attending a party were killed when caught in the cross-fire between two feuding gangs. After these tragic deaths, a number of politicians blamed gangsta rap for glamourising lawless lifestyles. But members of Black organisations claimed that it was poverty, unemployment and a sense of hopelessness that led some young Black men astray.

The Asian gang Clare Alexander (2000) studied a group of Bengali youngsters (mostly aged 14-16) in 'Stoneleigh' in inner-city London. She argues that the Asian 'gang' is largely a myth created after the riots in Northern England, and partly fuelled by a general rise in Islamophobia (hatred of Muslims). The mass media have circulated stories that Asian youth are gang members, criminals, school bullies and a major threat. But the reality is far more complex. Alexander admits that the Bengali youths often got involved in fighting, among themselves and against other ethnic groups. But she feels this was greatly exaggerated.

Also, she criticises the way teachers 'project' a gang structure on to Bengali youth – some teachers even claimed they knew the 'leaders', when in fact no leaders existed. Teachers believed all Bengalis have a common identity and a strong sense of belonging, and so they wrongly assumed they must stick together in gangs.

Youth gangs – conclusion

On the cinema screen gangs usually appear tightly organised and totally committed to criminal activity. But in real life what we call delinquent gangs are usually much more fleeting affairs, with casual membership and no binding rules.

This does not deny the existence of 'real' criminal behaviour among young people. The Milltown Boys did break the law frequently, and 'gangstas' are not totally imaginary. But sometimes the media build up a hype around youth crime and exaggerate its extent and intensity. They impose a structure on it which is not always justified.

key terms

Gang A group with a recognisable membership and tight structure, organised around criminal activities.
Territoriality A sense of 'ownership' over a geographical area, combined with a readiness to 'defend' it with force.
Delinquent subculture A way of life common among young people for whom delinquency is one, but not the only or main, activity.
Social network A loosely-organised grouping where people drift in and out.
Gangsta rap Themes within rap music which glamourise lawless behaviour and violent lifestyles.
Islamophobia Intense hatred of Muslims, based on exaggerated fears and stereotypes.

activity28 gangstas

Item A Street gangs

In England and Wales there may be as many as 30,000 members of violent street gangs engaged in drug dealing, robbery and even murder. Both victims and perpetrators are getting younger. The number of gang members under 16 has doubled in the past year and nearly half of all gang murders committed with firearms now involve victims under the age of 18.

The members listen to gangsta rap and idolise the heroes of films like *Scarface*, *Goodfellas* and *Menace 11 Society*. They talk about people getting 'jacked' (robbed or mugged), being 'blazed' (shot) and how they want 'the Cris life' (a reference to Cristal champagne, the ultimate in underworld chic).

Adapted from *The Observer*, 8.9.2002

Item B 50 Cent

questions

1 How does this article link gang membership with violence?
2 What image of gangstas is reflected in Item B?

summary

1. So-called youth gangs seldom have a recognised leader or fixed membership. They are more like social networks. There is not normally a shared commitment to delinquency, although some individuals do carve out criminal careers.

2. Membership of delinquent groups can give young people a sense of identity and support. They value the companionship of their friends. But over time many of them drift away from delinquent activities.

3. Claims about youth gangs are difficult to evaluate. Female delinquency appears to be on the increase, but it is unlikely there are many girls' gangs which exist for long or have a large membership. Likewise, Yardie-type 'gangsta' groups do exist, but it is difficult to estimate the numbers involved. The so-called Asian gangs are probably not nearly as widespread as some newspaper stories suggest.

Unit 7 Theories of delinquent subcultures

keyissues

1 What are the main functions of delinquent subcultures?

2 How do radicals explain delinquency?

3 Why are males more likely than females to commit delinquent acts?

There are likely to be differences in the motivations of twelve year-old kids who steal milk bottles, football hooligans who smash up trains, and teenagers who steal cars. But theories can help us understand some of the broad social reasons for the emergence and persistence of delinquent subcultures. In this unit we shall examine three major approaches: functionalist, radical and feminist. These theories have already been encountered in Unit 4. In many respects their explanations of delinquent subcultures are just a further spin on their views on youth subcultures in general, and the same criticisms usually apply.

Functionalist theories

Functionalists argue that youth subcultures arise because they help to solve some of the problems of youth. This is true of delinquent subcultures just as much as 'fun' subcultures. So the basic assumption is that delinquency is a problem-solving activity – joining the delinquent group provides a solution to certain problems faced by youth, especially working-class youth. This is an assumption that lies behind many of the 'classical' American theories of delinquent subcultures. We can understand it better if we look at two examples of these classical explanations.

Status frustration Albert Cohen (1955) argued that American society expects everyone to be successful – to get good jobs and earn plenty of money. Furthermore, it accepts no excuses for failure. Yet working-class kids grow up in more deprived circumstances and so they 'fail' more often. As a result, many of them suffer *status frustration* – they are not given status or respect by the rest of society, and they feel resentful about this. If this is the 'problem', then the 'solution' is to create their own game with its own rules, a game where they can win status on their own terms.

activity 29 belonging

The skinhead gang meets the needs of its members. It relieves them of boredom and gives them the excitement they seek. The conformity of the 'uniform' and the shared code of ideas and behaviour gives them identity and security. Belonging to the gang gives each member a status and a sense of being someone. It helps young men overcome their status frustration.

To all of the members, the gang itself had obviously been an invaluable experience. Our society usually sees gang structures as a threat and reacts against them. But the gang is a social structure which is formed by its members because they need it, because it may be their only form of defence or survival, and therefore it is valuable. The gang disappears as a gang when the members no longer need it.

Adapted from Daniel & McGuire, 1972

question

In what sense is this a 'functionalist' argument?

This game is delinquency, and it is one that is arrived at gradually through a series of minor delinquent escapades. Eventually the group may develop a full-blown delinquent subculture which rejects the values of respectable middle-class society. Within this subculture, the members can win status by expressing their delinquent values.

Lower class culture Walter Miller (1958) also adopts a 'functionalist' view but he takes a different tack from Cohen. According to Miller, working-class kids do not care much about what the middle class think of them. So delinquency is not a reaction to middle-class contempt. Rather, it is more or less the direct result of youngsters expressing lower-class values such as 'toughness' or 'excitement'. But where does the 'problem' appear in Miller's argument? Well, he argues that adolescence is a stage of life when people are unsure of themselves. So young people seek 'status' and need to feel they 'belong' to something. This leads to a delinquent solution. They can find a sense of belonging within the gang. And they can win status by expressing lower-class values. But because they are so keen to win acceptance from others, their behaviour has an air of desperation about it. So they exaggerate lower-class values and this spills over into delinquency. They show they are tough by fighting, and they find excitement by breaking laws.

Radical theories

Radicals point out that working-class youths are more likely to commit delinquent acts. No doubt there are biases in the official statistics (eg, student pranks are more likely to be overlooked). It is also true that class differences are a matter of degree (eg, middle-class youths take drugs too). Nevertheless, working-class youth have more powerful motives for delinquency.

Protest Radicals see delinquency as a disguised form of protest against capitalist society. They say it is in the nature of capitalism to create wide class and status inequalities and this increases the frustration and resentment of those who are at the bottom of the class pyramid. As a result, delinquent subcultures are bound to arise. Young people will be tempted to steal in order to get money. They will engage in 'expressive' acts of vandalism or violence as a way of venting their anger against the system. These delinquent subcultures can be seen as a form of symbolic resistance to the nature of capitalist society (compare 'resistance through 'rituals' on page 19). Delinquency is at heart a refusal to accept their subordinate position in society.

Scapegoating Of course, delinquency does not offer a direct challenge to capitalist society. It is a 'nuisance' rather than a form of 'political' opposition to powerful groups. Indeed, delinquency is often aimed at 'easy' targets – hippies, gays, ethnic minorities. These groups are used as scapegoats – they are blamed for problems (unemployment, poverty etc) which they did not cause. Instead of taking their anger out on politicians, skinheads go 'paki-bashing' or 'gay-bashing' or even fighting one another. So it is clear that delinquency is not usually a heroic act of resistance against an unjust society. It can take very unpleasant forms, where disadvantaged groups victimise other groups in society.

activity30 scapegoating

Item A Hardcore youth

'Having a skinhead haircut, the way you dress, you've made a vow to each other. You're hardcore. You're living it out. You're dedicated. You're living a life as a racist, patriot, nationalist, every minute of the day. Not when it suits you. When you look at us, you know what we are straightaway.'

A skinhead, quoted in Regan, 1993

Item B Rich hippies

'I hate them hippies. Them dirty 'ippies, poncing off us all the f...ing time. We 'ave to work and pay taxes and things, all these 'ippies are on the dole and don't do nothing and thieve and that. You notice that a lot of rich people turns 'ippie. They 'ave been spoilt. It's just to be the opposite of their parents, that's all it is.'

A skinhead, quoted in Daniel & McGuire, 1972

Item C A cautionary cartoon

questions

1 How do Items A and B show the 'scapegoating' nature of delinquency?
2 What warning is illustrated by the cartoon?

Feminist theories

Feminists note that criminologists neglected female offenders in the past and so they may have underestimated the extent of female delinquency. Feminists also complain that female delinquents are frequently stereotyped as 'pathological'. The commonsense assumption is that females are 'naturally' law-abiding and so any female offenders must have some abnormal biological or psychological problem. Against this, some feminists say that the explanation for gender differences in delinquency rates lies in the way girls are socialised into conformity. Females are subject to stricter social control and so it is more difficult for them to offend. However, gender roles in society are slowly changing and females are becoming more assertive and independent. Perhaps that is one reason why official statistics show an increase in female crime (although their rates are still well below those of males).

Warped masculinity Some feminists view delinquent subcultures as a warped expression of masculinity. For example, Beatrix Campbell (1993) describes how male youths make life miserable for others in the deprived estates of Britain. The riots in these estates in the early 1990s showed the differences in gender attitudes. While the women tried in vain to hold the communities together, young men were creating havoc and cowing neighbours into silence. Campbell believes masculinity is at the heart of the problem. The fathers of these unruly young men proved their masculinity by being breadwinners, but rising unemployment has blocked that route for many working-class youth. So these young men express their manhood in a violent and aggressive style. They define their masculinity by crime rather than work. Campbell cautions that she is not saying that boys are bad and girls are good, simply that they do different things to solve their troubles.

Theories of delinquent subcultures – conclusion

One of the striking things about these theories is how much they share in common. They see delinquency as the domain of young working-class males. They agree that these young men face certain problems which provide the motives for a delinquent 'solution'. This solution solves some problems although it may create others (eg, a criminal record will harm their employment prospects).

All these theories are pitched at a very general level. After all, only some working-class youths get involved in delinquency, only some males express their masculinity in violent ways. More detailed arguments are usually needed to help us understand why only some people take delinquent routes.

key terms

Status frustration The resentment felt by people who are denied status by society.
Scapegoat Persons or groups who are unfairly blamed for the faults of others or the problems of society.

activity31 riots

Item A You get respect

A discussion with some boys after the riots in Ely.

'I was throwing stones at the coppers because it was fun and everyone else was doing it.'

Did you want to hit the police?

'I didn't care.'

'I was throwing stones at the police because everybody was doing it. If it's happening it's worth doing it because you wouldn't want to be called a sap, would you?'

What does fighting achieve?

'Nothing really, it shows who is the hardest, so you get more respect.'

Who from?

'Other boys.'

Girls?

'They don't really matter.'

Adapted from Campbell, 1993

Item B Confrontation

Standing up to the police in Derry/Londonderry

question

What do these items indicate about the different attitudes of boys and girls?

summary

1. Functionalists argue that delinquent subcultures offer certain kinds of solutions for working-class youth. They provide them with a sense of 'belonging' to a group, and they allow them to win status through delinquent activity.

2. Radicals, too, argue that juvenile delinquency is largely a result of growing up in a class-divided society. Middle-class youths often have reasonable opportunities for 'getting on' and so they have a stake in conforming to society's norms. But working-class youths have less to lose by breaking the rules. Their delinquency is often a form of protest against the unfairness of society.

3. Feminists introduce gender into the argument. The poorer sections of society contain women as well as men. Yet it is largely men who commit delinquent acts. This suggests the importance of gender socialisation. Men are expected to be brave, active, strong – for some, delinquency may be the only way to express this.

Unit 8 Youth and schooling

keyissues

1. How is the experience of schooling affected by class, gender and ethnicity?

2. How is educational attainment affected by class, gender and ethnicity?

We spend many years of our lives in compulsory schooling. These school years are very important. We make friends in school, we get qualifications that set us on the pathway to jobs. But the experience of schooling is not the same for everyone – it is affected by our social class, gender and ethnicity.

Social class

Schools are divided along class lines in Britain. The rich and powerful elites pay hefty fees for their children to attend top public schools like Eton and Harrow. Here their children receive a highly privileged education and make valuable friendships which help them later in life when they need good 'contacts'. The children of middle-class parents may attend a 'minor' public school or be sent to a private school. Even if they attend a state school, their parents are in a good position to ensure this is a 'good' school. They can afford to move into the better residential areas where the local school has a good reputation. Working-class children usually have less scope for choice, and many of them end up in struggling 'sink' schools with poorer resources and a high turnover of teaching staff.

Class education There are broad differences in the educational profiles of different social classes. Working-class children are less likely to stay on when compulsory schooling ends (although the collapse of the youth labour

activity32 class divisions

Item A All-stars

In Eastford School there were class divisions among the girls. The elite 'all-stars' (academically gifted and socially prestigious) were aware of their envied position and looked down on the working-class girls who they dismissed as tarty 'fishwives' and 'slags'. In turn, the working-class girls regarded the elite as 'hippies' and 'snobs'.

Adapted from Hey, 1997

Item B Harrow public school

Item C State comprehensive

questions

1. Would Eastford school be the 'same' experience for these girls?

2. In what ways might the education of the young people in Items B and C differ?

market in recent years has encouraged more to stay on). Moreover, middle-class children are usually more successful in passing exams. There are a number of reasons for this. They may attend the 'better' schools and obviously that helps. Also, they have greater *economic capital* – their parents can afford to support them through a long education, buy them extra books and learning materials, and even pay for private tutors outside school. They also have higher *cultural capital* – their cultural background provides them with attitudes and values that equip them for educational success, and they are usually motivated and ambitious.

Learning to labour Some sociologists claim that schooling is a means by which pupils from different social classes are prepared for their respective roles in society. For example, Paul Willis (1977) followed 12 working-class boys (the 'lads') through their last few years at school. These boys developed disruptive styles – opposition to authority, ridicule of conformist pupils ('ear 'oles'), truancy, stealing (blagging) and 'having a laff'. These tactics helped them fight boredom and expressed their 'caged resentment' at their low educational status. But this response only locked them more firmly into a future of manual labour. The cultural values they prized – male bravado, toughness, an emphasis on the practical – prepared them for life on the factory floor. So ultimately they ended up in the same subordinate position as their parents.

Gender

Educational performance Feminists have documented how sexism within schools often held back the educational achievements of girls. For example, girls may have been discouraged from achieving educational success because their future was seen in terms of domestic roles such as housewife and mother, and/or low-skill, part-time jobs. However, times are changing along with gender differences in educational attainment. Girls have overtaken boys at every level – GCSE, A level and degree level.

Now there is increasing concern about 'underachieving' boys. This concern is perhaps exaggerated. Overall, the educational performance of *both* girls and boys is improving. It's just that girls have improved at a faster rate. However, the most recent available figures for GCSE (2003/04) show that the gender gap for A*-C grades narrowed slightly to 10 percentage points (DfES, 2005).

A number of reasons for the 'underperformance' of boys have been identified. These include the lack of role models (most teachers are female), the influence of 'lad culture' ('swots' are ridiculed) and low teacher expectations of boys. Girls, on the other hand, have increasing numbers of successful role models – the growing success of career women gives them an incentive to study harder. Girls nowadays want careers as well as marriage and children. Teachers also expect more of girls these days, so the culture of schools is changing.

Gender behaviour Within the classroom gender makes a difference. Boys tend to dominate classroom space – they talk more, they impose their physical presence and they are more likely to act the fool or mess about. Teachers tend to pay more attention to them (often to reprimand them rather than help them with their work). Griffin (1985) found that teachers expect boys to be disruptive and aggressive, but 'good' girls are quiet and obedient in class. Within the school playground and corridors, too, students behave in gendered ways, often sticking to same-sex groups. Of course, they interact too, and it is in these interactions that boys and girls build their different gender identities (they define themselves in comparison to each other). The sexually-charged atmosphere of school can make young people (especially girls) highly conscious of their 'sexual' reputations.

activity33 getting on

Item A Differences

It makes some difference whether your father is an unskilled manual worker or a well-paid professional, whether your parents showed an interest in your education, whether you attended a private school or a state comprehensive, whether you had your own bedroom in which to do your homework.

Adapted from Saunders, 1996

Item B Social class and exam results

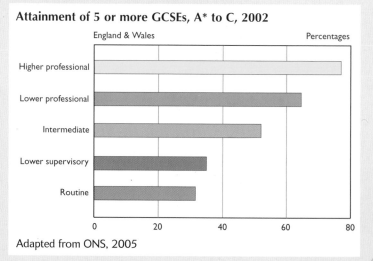

Attainment of 5 or more GCSEs, A* to C, 2002

England & Wales   Percentages

Adapted from ONS, 2005

question

Does Item B support the views in Item A?

activity34 the opposite sex

Item A Looking a prat

Frank: You want girls more than anything. You know we are always chasing them. We have all the pressure of having to get off with girls and asking them out.

Gilroy: That's true. It's the girls who have all the power. Like they have the choice and can make you look a prat in front of your mates.

Paul: You can't trust them. They talk to all their mates saying he's not very good and all. And they're really bitchy towards you and there's nothing you can do, coz you can't really hit a girl.

Adapted from Mac an Ghaill (1994)

Item B Problems with girls

question

How does the cartoon illustrate Item A?

Girls' friendship groups Sara Delamont (2001) says sociological research consistently shows the central importance of friendship groups to girls in school. Boys' friendship groups tend to be competitive and they avoid intimate talk. But girls frequently share confidences and intimate secrets with one another. Vivienne Griffiths (1995) studied girls' friendship groups in 'Barnsdale' High School, and found they could arouse fierce loyalties and strong divisions (eg, shutting out some girls). 'Falling out' with friends was a frequent event but it did not destroy the close and intense friendships. Griffiths takes a positive picture of these groups and she shows how they provide adolescent girls with a sense of power and self-esteem as well as fun.

Ethnicity

Ethnicity affects school experiences in various ways. It influences choice of schoolfriends – young people often hang around with people from the same ethnic group. There is also a possibility that the culture of the home clashes with the culture of the school. That is why some minority groups are keen on 'faith schools' where the atmosphere of the school takes fuller account of their cultural heritage. An additional problem is the ever-present threat of racial discrimination and prejudice within the school setting.

Ethnic performance Britain's ethnic minorities differ widely

activity35 ethnicity and educational attainment

Item A Exam results

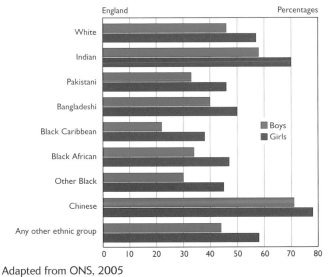

Attainment of 5 or more GCSEs, A* to C, 2002

Adapted from ONS, 2005

Item B Stereotypes

African-Caribbean boys are often stereotyped in terms of sport, music and crime. While they are seen as style leaders, their achievements are represented in terms of the 'body' rather than the 'mind'. As a result, many teachers have low academic expectations of them. Another problem is that African-Caribbean boys who study hard are often mocked by their peers – they are not seen as 'authentic' street-wise Blacks.

Adapted from Sewell, 1997

questions

1 What does the bar chart in Item A show?

2 How might Item B help explain the educational performance of African-Caribbean boys?

in their cultures and social class backgrounds. So it is hardly surprising that their educational performance varies. Within every ethnic group there are pupils who do well and pupils who perform poorly. But the 4th Survey by the Policy Studies Institute (Modood, 1997) found that the average performance of Chinese, African Asians and Indians is as good as, or better than, that of Whites. African-Caribbeans, Pakistanis and Bangladeshis do least well. Some educationalists explain this in terms of cultural differences. For example, 'Asian' cultures are seen as strong and supportive of educational success. But this stereotype does not explain the poor performance of Pakistanis and Bangladeshis.

Racism The school is a setting where ethnic minority pupils are likely to encounter racism. This could take the form of racial prejudice (negative attitudes) or racial discrimination (treating them differently). A report by the Commission for Racial Equality (1988) found that ethnic minority pupils are regularly subjected to bullying, taunts and name-calling in school playgrounds. Also, teachers have sometimes been accused of acting in a racist manner – they may hold rigid stereotypes of ethnic minority pupils and have different expectations of them. Asian pupils, for example, are commonly seen to be quiet and hard-working. But teachers sometimes have low expectations of African-Caribbean pupils, who they may see as idle and disruptive.

Youth and schooling – conclusion

Group characteristics do not seal the fate of school pupils. Within every group there are wide variations in attitudes and performance. Nevertheless, class, gender and ethnicity do affect how people feel about school, how they behave, how they are treated by others, and how they perform.

Another thing to remember is that class, gender and ethnicity interact. A girl is not just a girl, she is also a member of a social class and comes from a particular ethnic background. So the interplay of these factors has to be taken into account. For example, African-Caribbean girls have a better educational record than African-Caribbean boys.

key terms

Economic capital The economic resources which affect a social group's success.
Cultural capital The values, skills and motivation which affect a social group's success.
Lad culture The 'macho' values and lifestyles of boys, including an anti-learning attitude.
Racism A combination of negative attitudes and discriminatory treatment, aimed at ethnic minority groups.

summary

1. Middle-class pupils usually attend better schools and get better results. Schools help some working-class pupils get good educational qualifications and better jobs. But in some respects schools simply reproduce class divisions.

2. On average, girls do better than boys in terms of exam success. This may have something to do with their different attitudes and motivation. Behaviour in school varies along gender lines (eg, boys are more likely to clown around and misbehave).

3. There are wide variations in the educational performance of ethnic minority pupils. This partly reflects their different cultural attitudes and class backgrounds. In addition, it may be a result of racism within the school. Ethnic minority pupils may be racially harassed by other pupils, and teachers may hold misleading stereotypes about them.

Unit 9 Pro- and anti-school subcultures

keyissues

1　Why do pro- and anti-school subcultures emerge?

2　What are the main features of these subcultures?

School pupils develop different subcultures, including those which are distinctly pro- and anti-school – for and against school. David Hargreaves (1967) observed this process at work in 'Lumley School', and Colin Lacey (1970) identified a similar pattern in 'Hightown Grammar'. They describe the first year intake arriving fresh and eager and willing to work hard. But over the next few years there

is a process of 'differentiation' as the pupils are *streamed* (sorted into different classes according to their academic performance). This leads to 'polarisation' – the top academic streams become sharply divided from the bottom streams in terms of values and behaviour. The top streams work hard for academic success. They conform to 'middle class' values (ambition, planning ahead, respect for property). But the pupils in the lower streams gradually become disenchanted and form anti-school subcultures. They feel the teachers have little respect for them, and they have little incentive to prepare for exams. So they start 'playing up', breaking rules and engaging in petty delinquency.

activity36 attitudes

Item A Them and us

Attitudes of 'academic' pupils towards those below them

'I wouldn't want to be in their class – they're thick.'

'They are rough and tough.'

'I don't like them, they're a bit thick.'

'It's not easy to talk to them, they talk in a simpler way – they're only interested in football.'

Attitudes of 'non-academic' pupils to those above them

'They're not so friendly – they think they're better than us.'

'They are stuck up – because they think they are so brainy.'

'They're snobby, I don't like them.'

'They let you know they're in a higher class and how clever they are.'

Adapted from Ball, 1981

Item B Lumley School

question

How do Items A and B illustrate 'polarisation'?

Flexibility The early studies left the impression that pupils clearly belonged to either the pro- or the anti-school groups. But this 'bipolar model' was modified by later researchers who pointed to the existence of a mass of 'ordinary' kids somewhere between the two extremes. For example, Stephen Ball's (1981) study of 'Beachside Comprehensive' found an 'ambivalent' group who did not fit neatly into the pro- or anti-school camps. Also, the early studies seemed to imply that membership of the different groups was more or less fixed, with pupils behaving consistently according to the values of their respective groups. But later studies showed that many pupils were quite flexible in their attitudes and behaviour. David Gillborn's study (2002) of 'City Road Comprehensive' showed that pupils with high commitment to school occasionally play truant, while pupils in conflict with the school often comply with rules about attendance and school uniforms.

Parnell School

Many schools have introduced a vocational curriculum in order to help less academically gifted pupils develop job-oriented skills. Presumably this should weaken anti-school subcultures by giving those groups a bigger stake in school life. But Mac An Ghaill (1994) found that the mixture of academic and vocational routes still produces pro- and anti-school responses. In 'Parnell School', Mac an Ghaill found a wide range of what he calls 'fluid groups' (rather than tight subcultures). The main groups were as follows:

Ordinary Lads These were lads who belonged to non-academic peer groups. Their attitude to school was one of indifference, and they did not form a culture of resistance.

Macho Lads These were academic 'failures' who rejected the school's rules and regulations. Their values were 'looking after your mates', 'acting tough' and 'having a laugh'. They cultivated a masculine style based on physical courage (sticking up for yourselves), solidarity (sticking together) and territorial control (winning your own 'space'). They saw academic work as 'effeminate' and scorned the 'dickhead achievers' who studied hard.

Academic Achievers These were mainly from a skilled working-class background and they drew on a strong work ethic. They were not consistently pro-school but they tended to work hard.

New Enterprisers These were pupils who were enthusiastic about the new vocationally-oriented commercial and

activity37 truancy

'Bunking off' has a number of attractions. It is not just a matter of resistance to authority, or because school is so awful. It's also a valued activity in itself. Sometimes kids just prefer to enjoy the company of mates, watch afternoon television, have sex or adventures. Sometimes pupils play truant just so they won't be parted from their mates.

Adapted from Jenkins, 1983

question

How does this demonstrate the 'flexibility' of pupils?

technological subjects. They worked hard and they were critical of the Macho Lads' childish behaviour and low ability.

Real Englishmen This group had middle-class backgrounds and they were more confident and stylish than the other groups. They achieved academic success without seeming to work hard (unlike the Academic Achievers). They regarded the Macho Lads as trashy, vulgar and aggressive. However, like the Macho Lads they had little respect for their teachers, and this led them to challenge school rules.

activity38 heroes or villains?

Sociologists have glamourised the working-class boy who hates school, truants, avoids his school work, and copies and cheats when he does complete it. They treat him as a sort of 'hero'. Yet these boys make life very difficult for their teachers and for other pupils. They despise hard-working boys as effeminate and weak. They gain status from boasting of their sexual conquests and delinquent activities. They are often sexist and racist, and they value fighting and toughness.

Adapted from Delamont, 2000

question

Which group in Parnell school most closely resembles these 'heroes'?

Ethnic subcultures

Teacher stereotypes Gillborn's study (2002) of 'City Road Comprehensive' indicates that teachers operated with stereotypes of ethnic minority pupils. They had low expectations of Black pupils and criticised them frequently (and often on the grounds of their 'manner' or 'bad attitude' rather than their actual behaviour). Any expression of Black cultural style (eg, walking with an exaggerated swing of the shoulders, or talking in dialect) was seen as a 'threat'. The teachers were *ethnocentric* (blinkered by their own cultural assumptions) and so they were unable to understand or sympathise with the cultural differences of Black pupils.

Although Asian pupils were culturally different they presented fewer problems. Teachers saw Asians as quiet, well-behaved, highly motivated and coming from supportive family backgrounds. Generally speaking, teachers were more sympathetic to Asian cultural diversity (eg, Asian females were the only female pupils exempt from wearing skirts to school).

activity39 stereotypes

Tony Sewell interviewing Mr S, a teacher at Township School

Mr S: I've really tried hard with Errol but he's a bloody waste of time.

TS: What about his parents?

Mr S: Well, you only have to look at his Dad to see what home he comes from. He comes into school very cocky dripping with gold chains and a flash car.

TS: What do you mean?

Mr S: Well, he looks like a gangster or drug-dealer.

TS: How would you describe your relationship with the parents of African-Caribbean boys?

Mr S: I have talked to many parents who share my cultural values.

TS: Which are?

Mr S: They believe in courtesy, they believe in looking smart, working hard, ambition, and accepting authority. Sadly, there are other parents who don't share these values and it shows in the behaviour of their children. These parents usually get aggressive when the school punishes their child.

Adapted from Sewell, 1997

question

What stereotypes are expressed in this interview?

Black responses Sewell (1997) found a range of styles adopted by the African-Caribbean boys in the two schools he studied. These included hard-working 'conformists' (the largest single group), 'retreatists' (a small group who rejected schoolwork but did not have a subcultural alternative), and 'rebels' (deeply involved in ragga culture). The rebels were the most visible anti-school subculture and they placed great emphasis on sexual reputation, physical

activity40 real Englishmen

Interviews with White 'Real Englishmen' in Parnell school

Adam: It's like we can't be English, English men, be proud of being English. I argue about this with my dad all the time.

Mac an Ghaill: Why is it important to you?

Adam: Because it's unfair. All the Asian kids and the Black kids, they can be Asian or Black. They can be proud of their countries.

Mac an Ghaill: Do you think of yourselves as racist?

Adam: No. No. That's what the teachers try and tell you, they try and force on you if you say anything, try to make you feel guilty like them. But we're not talking about colour. We're talking about culture.

Richard: English culture. And if you talk about the English flag or whatever, anything to do with Englishness, they call you a little fascist.

Adapted from Mac an Ghaill, 1994

question

What does this reveal about tensions between ethnic groups in schools?

---

strength and violence. Schoolwork was seen as a threat to their 'manhood'.

These rebels resemble the 'Rasta Heads' identified by Mac an Ghaill (1988) in 'Kilby' inner-city school. The Rasta Heads developed a culture of resistance modelled on Rastafarian dress codes and hairstyles, and they adopted 'ethnic' ways of moving and speaking. These boys were disruptive: they arrived late for classes, demanded their seats at the back, talked during lessons and refused to apologise when reprimanded. Although the group included academically talented boys, they were under-achievers in examinations.

Asian resistance Mac an Ghaill also identified an Asian group – the 'Warriors' – in Kilby school. Although this group displayed an anti-school and anti-racist stance, their resistance was largely 'invisible' to the teachers. Blinded by stereotypes of the 'good' Asian pupil, the teachers saw them as 'middle class' and 'conformist', even though they were a tough and violent group who were feared within the school. Any misbehaviour by a Warrior was seen as an 'individual' affair rather than typical behaviour by Asian pupils.

Girls' subcultures

Girls make few appearances in the literature on anti-school subcultures. Both Griffin (1985) and Griffiths (1995) found it difficult to identify clear-cut pro- and anti-school subcultures among girls. Studies of girls seldom find the polarisation that exists among boys. In 'Barnsdale' school, Griffiths found that girls who were struggling academically still continued to study reasonably hard and usually gave little trouble to teachers.

When girls feel resentment against the school, this is less likely to take the form of open challenge and unruly conduct. Rather, it is more likely to be expressed in an exaggerated display of 'femininity' and 'sexuality' (eg, girls may show their disenchantment with the school by wearing make-up, short skirts, fancy hairdos). But this emphasis on femininity does not necessarily clash with academic study. For example, Griffiths found it was possible for girls to combine an interest in femininity

activity41 notes

The notes that girls pass to one another in class are often regarded by teachers as silly or mischievous. But girls put a great deal of effort into them and they are a major way of maintaining friendships. The girls also use them as a way of resisting pressure to 'be nice' – in the notes they gossip, bitch, banter and make fun of each other.

Adapted from Hey, 1997

question

How do the notes help girls to resist their 'good' image?

with good academic achievement and a pro-school attitude.

Girls' resistance Organised anti-school subcultures may not be highly visible among girls but they often manage to resist teachers' demands in more subtle ways. Griffiths (1995) describes the various 'little' forms of resistance that girls adopt. These include day-dreaming in class, writing on desks or on books, combing or sucking hair, reading magazines in class, passing notes to each other, being slow or late, sullen resentment, cheeking teachers, teasing, humour, altering their uniform, talking in class, truanting, and 'making space' (eg, creating their own smoking areas).

Black Sisters Mac an Ghaill (1988) studied the 'Black Sisters', a group of 6th form pupils at 'Connolly School'. He describes their opposition as taking the form of 'resistance within accommodation'. Proud to be Black and female, they rejected any image of themselves as 'conformist' or 'passive'. In many small ways they tried to oppose what they saw as the racism of the school. Yet this resistance was accompanied by a certain amount of 'accommodation' too. They managed to avoid open conflict with teachers. Also, although they were anti-school they remained pro-education, and they worked hard for academic success.

Pro- and anti-school subcultures – conclusion

Anti-school subcultures are a favourite topic in educational research. Indeed, Sara Delamont (2000) criticises researchers for glamourising working-class boys as 'heroes' on account of their resistance to a school system which labels them as failures.

However, there has been a switch away from working-class males towards studies of girls and ethnic minorities. The introduction of gender issues and racist stereotypes creates a much more complex picture. For example, it appears there is no inevitable link between anti-school attitudes and educational success.

key terms

Anti-school subcultures The subcultures of groups who oppose or resist school values, rules and regulations.
Pro-school subcultures The subcultures of groups who support school values, rules and regulations.
Bipolar model The view that school pupils tend to separate into two opposed groups, the pro- and anti-school subcultures.
Streaming The separation of school pupils according to their academic performance.
Ethnocentrism Cultural short-sightedness – a failure to understand other cultures.

summary

1. Academic streaming within schools can lead to the formation of pro- and anti-school subcultures. But research suggests the existence of additional groups who do not fit these two extremes. Also, attitudes to school are not fixed – pupils may shift between pro- and anti- stances at different times.

2. Girls tend to show their resistance to school not through openly disruptive behaviour but in more disguised forms (eg, passing notes, or gentle testing of the school's rules on things like uniform or make-up).

3. Anti-school subcultures are found among ethnic minorities, especially African-Caribbeans. In part, this is a response to what they see as racism and ethnocentrism within the school. Teachers may hold stereotypes of minority pupils – the 'troublesome' African-Caribbean, the 'good' Asian. These stereotypes affect interactions between teachers and pupils.

4. There is no direct link between attitudes to school and educational performance. For example, some young African-Caribbean women may not be 'model' pupils. They may appear uninterested during lessons and they may have little affection for school or teachers. But this does not necessarily prevent them from studying hard and passing exams.

Unit 10 *Masculinity, femininity and school*

keyissues

1 How are gender identities created in schools?
2 What effect does gender have on subject choice?

Creating identities

Schools are gendered institutions in the sense that boys and girls tend to have different roles and expectations within them. In some ways this reflects the gender identities and stereotypes that operate outside schools. But

Mac an Ghaill (1994) argues that schools are also where young people learn to build and create their gender identities. Mac an Ghaill's study of 'Parnell School' suggests that schools can produce a range of masculinities and femininities. In other words, there is no single masculine or feminine identity. Rather, young people find and create different subcultural versions (eg, some boys build 'sporty' identities, others create 'arty' identities). Nevertheless, there are some dominant assumptions about gender which limit the choices (eg, it is assumed that heterosexuality is the only 'normal' sexual orientation, and this makes life difficult for gay pupils).

Adolescents and sexuality

Boys Holland et al. (1998) show how boys build up a sense of their sexuality as they interact with other schoolfriends. They learn what makes them attractive or otherwise to the opposite sex (spotty and shy youths are seen as less 'manly'). They learn masculine 'scripts' by listening to and telling 'sexual performance' stories (eg, boasts about who did what to whom, who pulls all the girls etc). This teaches them to distinguish between 'wimps' and 'gladiators'. Scared of being seen as a wimp, young men set out to prove their masculinity. Often this means acting tough and aggressive, being competitive, looking down on gays and treating girls as 'fair game'.

Girls Valerie Hey (1997) describes the social and sexual competition among girls in a couple of London schools. The girls were constantly trying to prove to one another that they were 'normal' girls. They tried to construct a 'feminine' identity for themselves and they attached negative labels ('slags', 'dykes') to girls who strayed too far

from this identity. Hey argues that these girls simply end up controlling each other's behaviour in unhealthy ways. Also, by defining themselves in terms of their 'femininity' they link their identity too closely to boys' opinion of them.

However, research by Sue Lees (1993) suggests that girls no longer passively accept their 'subordinate' role to boys. They are starting to question sexism and they are teasing each other for playing up to boys. Instead of being anxious about what boys think of them, girls are becoming more self-assured and more confident about their own sexual identities.

Subject choice

Another way in which young people express their gender identities is in choice of school subjects. At one time it was common for boys and girls to study different subjects (eg, woodwork for boys, domestic science for girls). Modern curriculum design has broken down many of these traditional gender divisions, with both sexes being required to take the same subjects. Nevertheless, pupils still have some measure of choice, especially in the later years at school. Moreover, some school subjects still have a reputation as 'masculine' or 'feminine' and so we find some subjects are dominated by one sex.

In the 1990s, for example, boys were still more likely to take physics, design and technology, and computer studies, while girls were more likely to take subjects such as French or biology. There are signs of growing gender equality in GCSE subjects such as maths, English and modern languages, but differences become more marked at A level. These gender-based choices have an influence on the types of careers or higher education courses young people can pursue. Yet sometimes young people just 'drift' into certain subjects because of their masculine or feminine images.

activity42 weapons

If teenage girls want to bring another girl into line, they are unlikely to thump her into submission. They'll just erode her self-confidence.

All those little adolescent taunts – 'How come you don't have a boyfriend? How come you don't have any decent clothes?' – are more effective than a thousand beatings.

There's other weaponry too: ostracism ('Sorry we didn't invite you to the party – you wouldn't have liked it'), slurs ('She's just after your man') and friendly advice ('Don't worry, you've just got big bones').

Girls are good at detecting the weak spots and then exploiting them. They also manage a double-edged morality, being both obsessed with sex and yet giving each other a hard time for having it. 'She's a slag/slapper/tart' isn't only something that boys say.

Adapted from Bathurst, 2002

question

What does this reveal about competition between girls?

Table 5 *Examination entries 1999/2000*

GCSE/SCE	Girls (thousands)	Boys (thousands)
English	325	323
French	197	179
Mathematics	333	338
Computer studies	47	72
Geography	115	149
Art & Design	119	98
Design & Technology	210	244
Science double award	250	244
GCE A level/SCE Higher		
English	29	18
English Literature	45	19
French	15	6
Mathematics	34	51
Biology	39	23
Physics	10	31
Art & Design	27	15
Geography	21	25

Adapted from Equal Opportunities Commission, 2002

activity43 *gender subjects*

Item A *Images*

One of the reasons boys do not do as well as girls in English is because of their attitudes to the subject. Boys see English as a 'feminine' subject that is alien to their way of thinking and working. They feel 'uncomfortable' in English, whereas they feel 'safe' in science:

'Science is straightforward. You don't have to think about it. There are definite answers. But English is about understanding, interpreting, you have to think more. There's no definite answer, the answer depends on your view of things.'

   This research evidence suggests that boys' views are related to the position of men in society. Men have to be seen as strong, sure of themselves, and always in control. Women are seen as the 'understanding', 'caring' sex and they don't mind getting it wrong.

Adapted from Mitsos, 1995

Item B *English literature*

question
What do these items reveal about gender attitudes in school?

Masculinity, femininity and school – conclusion

The secondary school years are a time when young people become much more concerned about their sexual and gender identities. Of course, they already have some idea of society's gender stereotypes and expectations. But it is within the school that they start to build a much more detailed sense of their own identities. Interacting with other pupils, they learn which sorts of identities are seen as 'normal', which types of sexual behaviour are admired or condemned.

   Gender assumptions also enter into the choice of school subjects. Subjects which require 'logic' are stereotyped as 'masculine', and those which require verbal fluency and interpretation as 'feminine'. Also, subjects become 'gendered' according to who teaches them (physics teachers tend to be male, biology teachers female). But these assumptions seem to be changing, however slowly.

key terms

Sexism Treating people in terms of gender stereotypes, when gender is not really a relevant issue.
Sexual performance stories Stories that celebrate the sexual attractiveness and success of the story-teller (usually male!).

summary

1. Boys and girls work out their gender identities and sexuality within the school. A range of identities are created but some are dominant (eg, assumptions about the normality of heterosexuality). Boys are often under pressure to prove their masculine virility, and girls often have to defend their reputation. But some researchers detect signs of more relaxed and less stereotyped attitudes in recent years.

2. Schools no longer enforce rigid gender divisions. As a result, gender divisions in subjects are not as marked as in the past. But some differences still exist. This is partly because certain subjects have a gender 'image'.

References

Alexander, C. (2000). *The Asian gang.* Oxford: Berg.

Aries, P. (1962). *Centuries of childhood.* London: Cape.

Back, L. & Keith, M. (1999). Rights and wrongs. In P. Cohen (Ed.), *New ethnicities, old racisms.* London: Zed Books.

Ball, S.J. (1981). *Beachside comprehensive.* Cambridge: Cambridge University Press.

Bathurst, B. (2002). Isn't it clever and isn't it fun. *The Guardian*, 30 September.

Beaumont, P. (1996). Thirty-somethings who won't grow up. *The Observer*, 19th May.

Bennett, A. (1999). Subcultures or neo-tribes. *Sociology, 33*, 3.

Bennett, A. (2001). *Cultures of popular music.* Buckingham: Open University Press.

Berger, B. (1971). *Looking for America.* New Jersey: Prentice-Hall.

Bradford, S. & Urquhart, C. (1998). The making and breaking of young men. *Youth and Policy, 61.*

Brinkworth, L. (1997). Twisted sisters. *Harpers & Queen.* April.

Campbell, B. (1993). *Goliath.* London: Methuen.

Cieslik, M. & Pollock, G. (2002). *Young people in risk society.* Aldershot: Ashgate.

Cohen, A. (1955). *Delinquent boys.* Glencoe: Free Press.

Cohen, P. (1972). Subcultural conflict and working class community. *Working Papers in Cultural Studies, 2.*

Cohen, S. (1987). *Folk devils and moral panics* (2nd ed.). Oxford: Blackwell.

Cohen, P. (1997). *Rethinking the youth question.* Basingstoke: Macmillan.

Coward, R. (1999). *Sacred cows.* London: Harper Collins.

Commission for Racial Equality (1988). *Learning in terror.* London: CRE.

Daniel, P. & McGuire, S. (1972). *Paint house.* Harmondsworth: Penguin.

Delamont, S. (2000). The anomalous beasts. *Sociology, 34*, 1.

Delamont, S. (2001). *Changing women, unchanged men?* Buckingham: Open University Press.

Equal Opportunities Commission (2002). *Facts about men and women in Great Britain.* London: EOC.

Furlong, A. & Cartmel, F. (1997). *Young people and social change.* Philadelphia: Open University Press.

Garratt, D., Roche, J. & Tucker, S. (1997). *Changing experiences of youth.* London: Sage.

Gillborn, D. (2002). *Ethnicity and education.* London: RoutledgeFalmer.

Gordon, P. & Rosenberg, D. (1989). *Daily racism.* London: Runnymede Trust.

Graham, J. & Bowling, B. (1995). *Young people and crime.* London: Home Office.

Griffin, C. (1985). *Typical Girls.* London: Routledge.

Griffiths, V. (1995). *Adolescent girls and their friends.* Aldershot: Avebury.

Hall, S., Critcher, C., Jefferson, T., Clarke, J. & Roberts, B. (1978). *Policing the crisis.* London: Macmillan.

Hargreaves, D. (1967). *Social relations in a secondary school.* London: Routledge & Kegan Paul.

Heidensohn, F. (2002). Gender and crime. In M. Maguire, R. Morgan & R. Reiner (Eds.), *The Oxford handbook of criminology.* Oxford: Oxford University Press.

Hey, V. (1997). *The company she keeps.* Buckingham: Open University Press.

Hobbs, D. (1988). *Doing the business.* Oxford: Clarendon Press.

Hodkinson, P. (2002). *Goth.* Oxford: Berg.

Holland, J., Ramazanoglu, C., Sharpe, S. & Thomson, R. (1998). *The male in the head.* London: Tufnell Press.

Jefferson, T. (Ed.) (1975). *Resistance through rituals.* Birmingham: Centre for Contemporary Cultural Studies.

Jenkins, R. (1983). *Lads, citizens and ordinary kids.* London: Routledge & Kegan Paul.

Katz, A. (1997). *The can-do girls.* Oxford University: Dept of Applied Social Studies & Research.

Katz, A. (1999). *The leading lads.* Oxford University: Dept of Applied Social Studies & Research.

Lacey, C. (1970). *Hightown grammar.* Manchester: Manchester University Press.

Leech, K. (1976). *Youthquake.* London: Abacus.

Lees, S. (1993). *Sugar and spice.* Harmondsworth: Penguin.

Mac an Ghaill, M. (1988). *Young, gifted and Black.* Milton Keynes: Open University Press.

Mac an Ghaill, M. (1994). *The making of men.* Buckingham: Open University Press.

Macpherson, Sir Wm. (1999). *The Stephen Lawrence report.* London: HMSO.

Maguire, M. (2002). Crime statistics. In M. Maguire, R. Morgan & R. Reiner (Eds.), *The Oxford handbook of criminology.* Oxford: Oxford University Press.

McRobbie, A. (1991). *Feminism and youth culture.* London: MacMillan.

McRobbie, A. & Garber, J. (1975). Girls and subcultures. In T. Jefferson (Ed.), *Resistance through rituals.* Birmingham University: Centre for contemporary cultural studies.

Mead, M. (1977). *Coming of age in Samoa.* Harmondsworth: Penguin. (originally published 1928).

Miller, W. (1958). Lower class culture as a generating milieu of gang delinquency. *Journal of Social Issues, 14.*

Mitsos, E. (1995). Classroom voices. *The English and media magazine, 33,* 34.

Modood, T. (1997). *Ethnic minorities in Britain.* London: Policy Studies Institute.

Morgan, P. (1978). *Delinquent fantasies.* London: Temple Smith.

Muncie, J. (1999). *Youth and crime.* London: Sage.

Murdock, G. & McCrone, R. (1975). Consciousness of class and consciousness of generation. In T. Jefferson (Ed.), *Resistance through rituals.* Birmingham: Centre for contemporary cultural studies.

Newburn, T. (2002). Young people, crime and youth justice. In M. Maguire, R. Morgan & R. Reiner (Eds.), *The Oxford handbook of criminology.* Oxford: Oxford University Press.

Osgerby, B. (1998). *Youth in Britain since 1945.* Oxford: Blackwell.

Parker, H. Williams, L. & Aldredge, J. (2002). The normalisation of 'sensible' recreational drug use. *Sociology, 36*, 4.

Parsons, T. (1954). *Essays in sociological theory.* Glencoe: Free Press.

Patrick, J. (1973). *A Glasgow gang observed.* London: Methuen.

Pearson, G. (1983). *Hooligan.* Basingstoke: Macmillan.

Pilcher, J. (1995). *Age and generation in modern Britain*. Oxford: Oxford University Press.

Polhemus, T. (1997). In the supermarket of style. In S. Redhead (Ed.), *The clubcultures reader*. Oxford: Blackwell.

Postman, N. (1983). *The disappearance of childhood*. London: W.H. Allen.

Power, A. & Tunstall, R. (1997). *Dangerous disorder*. York: Joseph Rowntree Foundation.

Regan, L. (1993). *Public enemies*. London: Andre Deutsch.

Richards, A. (1982). *Chisunga*. London: Tavistock.

Roberts, H. & Sachdev, D. (1996). *Having their say*. Ilford: Barnardo's.

Roberts, K. (1997). Same activities, different meanings. *Leisure Studies, 16*.

Roberts, R. (1971). *The classic slum*. Harmondsworth: Penguin.

Saunders, P. (1996). *Unequal but fair*. London: IEA.

Sewell, T. (1997). *Black masculinities and schooling*. Stoke on Trent: Trentham Books.

Taylor, I. (1997). Running on empty. *The Guardian*, 14 May.

Thornton, S. (1995). *Club cultures*. Cambridge: Polity Press.

Thrasher, F. (1927). *The gang*. Chicago: Chicago University Press.

Tucker, N. (1998). More sex please, we're British. *Guardian Education*, 14 April.

Wardak, A. (2000). *Social control and deviance*. Aldershot: Ashgate.

Williamson, H. (1997a) Status Zer0 youth and the 'underclass'. In R. MacDonald (Ed.), *Youth, the 'underclass' and social exclusion*. London: Routledge.

Williamson, H. (1997b). *Youth and policy*. Aldershot: Ashgate.

Williamson, H. (2001). *The Milltown Boys*. Leicester: National Youth Agency.

Willis, P. (1977). *Learning to labour*. Farnborough: Gower.

Wiseman, C.V., Gray, J.J., Mosimann, J.E. & Ahrens, A.H. (1992). Cultural expectations of thinness in women: An update. *International Journal of Eating Disorders, 11*, 85-89.

Author index

Subject index